Literacy Learning Journeys

As educators, we want to help our learners flourish during their time with us, both academically and socially. However, many dyslexic children and young people experience substantial barriers to accessing the curriculum which can impact both their academic progress and overall wellbeing.

This easy-to-read book equips educators with essential knowledge and practical guidance to ensure that all dyslexic students can access the curriculum effectively and fully express their ideas, creativity and understanding. Drawing on research and the author's extensive experience, the book includes:

- A comprehensive introduction to dyslexia and an overview of what it can look like at different stages of education, from the Early Years to Year 11 and beyond.

- Practical, evidence-based strategies to help students with dyslexia and specific literacy difficulties engage with the curriculum, make progress and enjoy learning across their entire educational journey.

- A wealth of case studies and interview excerpts from students, parents and teachers to contextualise their experiences.

- Reflection prompts and exercises to help you consider your own learners so that you can draw on strategies presented in this book as part of your own practice.

Literacy Learning Journeys champions kindness and empathy and takes a positive approach to dyslexia to help children and young people thrive in the mainstream classroom. With easy to dip in and out chapters and signposting to further reading and resources, it is essential reading for teachers, teaching assistants and anyone working with learners with dyslexia.

Helen Ross is a Special Educational Needs specialist and dyslexia expert. She founded Helen's Place to support young people to be their best 'selves' through holistic intervention, focussing on building positive working relationships with all stakeholders of their education. Helen is also Chair of the Wiltshire Dyslexia Association, supporting events, providing advice on pedagogy and contributing to the association's social media networks. She has worked extensively with the British Dyslexia Association and other third-sector organisations, aiming to continue supporting people with dyslexia and make the world a more inclusive place.

Literacy Learning Journeys

An Educator's Guide to Dyslexia,

Ages 0–18

Helen Ross

Routledge
Taylor & Francis Group

LONDON AND NEW YORK

Designed cover image: Getty Images

First published 2025
by Routledge
4 Park Square, Milton Park, Abingdon, Oxon OX14 4RN

and by Routledge
605 Third Avenue, New York, NY 10158

Routledge is an imprint of the Taylor & Francis Group, an informa business

© 2025 Helen Ross

The right of Helen Ross to be identified as author of this work has been asserted in accordance with sections 77 and 78 of the Copyright, Designs and Patents Act 1988.

All rights reserved. No part of this book may be reprinted or reproduced or utilised in any form or by any electronic, mechanical, or other means, now known or hereafter invented, including photocopying and recording, or in any information storage or retrieval system, without permission in writing from the publishers.

Trademark notice: Product or corporate names may be trademarks or registered trademarks, and are used only for identification and explanation without intent to infringe.

British Library Cataloguing-in-Publication Data
A catalogue record for this book is available from the British Library

ISBN: 9781032660400 (hbk)
ISBN: 9781032659046 (pbk)
ISBN: 9781032660417 (ebk)

DOI: 10.4324/9781032660417

Typeset in Optima
by Deanta Global Publishing Services, Chennai, India

Contents

Acknowledgements — vii

Introduction — 1

1 Neurodiversity: A Brief History and Overview — 7

2 Dyslexia: More Than Just a Reading Problem — 15

3 Dyslexia in the Early Years — 31

4 Dyslexia in Early Primary School — 50

5 Dyslexia in Later Primary School — 76

6 Secondary School — 104

7 Children, Teachers and Family: The Stakeholder Triad — 133

8 Life After School — 152

9 Concluding Thoughts and Further Reading — 176

Index — 199

Acknowledgements

There are a lot of people who stand behind me, propping me up and picking me up off the floor when I have a strop, or a crisis of confidence. I hope that I have thanked them all personally and if I haven't, I will next time I see you. There are a few people who need personal mentions as they are particularly important in my little world.

Firstly, Mr Dr Ross. That rare nexus between brave, stupid and patient: you are all of those things and all of those things have been tested during the process of this book, as well as every single day of your life! I appreciate you very much. Thank you for all you are, all you do, and all you support me to be and do.

The Little Dude, for being a little star and just making me smile when I need it and he makes me proud every blooming day. And I don't share cake, unless I'm broken!!

Lucy P, amazing lady that you are. You are much appreciated and I love that you are on the end of the phone when I need it. You let me cry, rant and laugh with you and for that, you are amazing!

Michael D, thank you for knowing when to be daft, say something nice and to generally let me prattle on whenever I need to. You are immensely appreciated!

Victoria AP, thank you. Thank you for your kindness and poo-sandwiches with my drawings and for just getting it! After 35 years, you are so valued!

Georgina D, this is all your fault and for that, I thank you! You are inspirational, knowledgeable and just blooming amazing.

Last but not least, thank you to the kind and amazing people who have shared their stories and journeys with me as I have worked on this book. I literally could not have done it without your input. I actively haven't named you in the process, because for some people it was important to respect their privacy. I value your contributions to this book and appreciate

Acknowledgements

what you've shared. I wish all of you well as you and your families move forward. Thank you!

Introduction

Dyslexia in a Crowded System

In a system where educators are being asked to support learners with increasingly complex needs in the mainstream classroom, invisible needs such as dyslexia can often go under the radar. Young people with dyslexia don't always stand out readily; you can't see dyslexia but it is present in every classroom in the UK today with an estimated one in ten people having dyslexia. This means that every teacher will be working with dyslexic children, but they may not know it or may not feel that they are confident in explicitly addressing children's needs. The current Special Educational Needs and Disability (SEND) system seems to be evermore pressed and consistently under-resourced. This leaves classroom teachers often working with complex students whose needs may be more 'obvious', and those teachers then feel that they don't have capacity or support to be able to meet the needs of children with dyslexia or other literacy challenges.

Dyslexia is a contested phenomenon; there is no single, approved and agreed definition of it and the debate as to its existence surfaces periodically. Even during the writing of this book, a new conceptualisation of dyslexia was released based on substantial and in-depth research. This and other definitions of dyslexia are discussed in detail later, but in broad strokes, dyslexia is linked to challenges in phonological awareness (manipulating speech sounds), verbal processing (filing and accessing language-based information between long- and short-term memory) and working memory. These vulnerabilities then impact on academic attainment, often affecting literacy most strongly but sometimes also affecting other areas, such as numeracy.

Teachers need to understand the experiences of dyslexic children and know how they can tweak their lesson delivery so that dyslexic children can better access learning. But this has also got to be doable without overloading teachers with extra tasks and papers to drown under! Dyslexia is in the mainstream classroom to stay, so I want to help teachers know what they can do to support children within their own planning.

What Are We Aiming For

This book aims to give you an overview of what dyslexia looks like at different stages in a child's education, linking to the evolving changes in curriculum expectations. The book gives you opportunities to look beyond your own training and to see what happens at different points along a child's journey through school so you can see what precedes your teaching stage and what comes next. We give you 'reflection points' throughout the book, with questions, things to consider and some examples to help guide your thinking. We link to policy, and contextualise this within wider literature, drawing mainly on English frameworks but also linking to the Welsh, Scottish and Northern Irish contexts. A variety of case studies are also presented, drawing on both well-known individuals and families/professionals I met in the process of preparing this book. All of these are linked to resources and suggested strategies to support dyslexic children across their educational journey. In writing this book, I aim to provide practical and straightforward strategies to support children academically, whilst empowering you to better understand their wider experiences.

You may choose to read the book from cover to cover, or you may find that it's most useful as a reference guide that you dip in and out of. The key thing is that you will feel more confident and knowledgeable after you have read the book!

How the Book Was Written

This book aims to be wholly accessible, uplifting voices from people who are affected by dyslexia and literacy difficulties whether in their professional lives, or their personal lives, as educators, parents, dyslexics or others who advocate for, and work within the dyslexia community. The book does not aim to give generalisable strategies that have been gained through large survey data, or from reading secondhand data, or working remotely or talking to people on the front line in the dyslexia community. A collaborative approach was taken in the research and preparation of this book, which aligns with the underpinning frameworks I use in my more formal academic and research work.

During the summer of 2023, I put requests for people to come forward on social media if they or members of their family/household were able to and felt comfortable to share some of their experiences with me in an interview. I devised interview schedules for parents/carers, young people and educators, as well as other interested adults, that explored people's experiences of dyslexia in school. The questions touched on when people's dyslexia was identified, how it affected them (or their children) in school, what was done about it, and what they have done subsequently, either in spite of or thanks to their dyslexia. A broad range of people replied to the request and I was very privileged to be entrusted with sharing their stories. While some people were happy for me to share their identity in this process, others were not, so I have anonymised all the names and locations of people I spoke to in the process. This reflects good practice in research, to ensure the wellbeing of participants.

Once I had interviewed people, I transcribed the interviews, removing any identifiable features and looking for themes in the different transcripts as they linked to the chapters in the book. I used the interviews to help generate case studies, support and intervention strategy suggestions, and examples of how dyslexia can appear, as well as inform, the contents of the reflection point boxes which appear throughout the book. Wider research was carried out from academic journals and professional publications as well as government resources. A wide range of different sources were used to reflect the broad range of stakeholder individuals and organisations connected with dyslexia in the UK.

A Walk Through the Chapters

The book has nine chapters and they all cover different elements of dyslexia in the education system. An overview of the chapters is given here so that you know broadly what to expect from them all, when you pick up the book. Worry not though – you don't have to read a whole chapter; you may find that just a small section is helpful for you at any given moment. Each chapter has a similar structure, with references, further reading and Key Takeaways so that you can read more about given topics if you want to, using the sources signposted.

Chapter 1 sets the scene for the field of neurodiversity. Dyslexia sits within the range of neurodiversities, but the term was coined within the autistic community and used to frame the different ways in which they process the world positively. The term is unpacked here, then I explain how dyslexia fits into the paradigm.

Dyslexia and what it means is explored in Chapter 2. There have been many different definitions and explanations of it from 'word blindness' to sophisticated and multi-faceted models where vulnerabilities in cognitive processing are linked to challenges in academic attainment. Whilst I was writing this book, a new conceptualisation of dyslexia was published and this has been included here. I also highlight some of the policy frameworks which are implicated in working with dyslexic children, as they progress through education.

In Chapter 3, we start to look at how dyslexia can appear in different stages of a child's educational journey. Although it is not generally assessed before a child is seven, there can be signs of potential dyslexia very early in their life. Here, we look at the Early Years and Foundation Stage, and what children are expected to do at each point. How dyslexia may look for children at those points is linked to the curriculum, with simple activities suggested to help pinpoint young children's needs and how to support them.

Chapter 4 moves along to Key Stage 1, highlighting the different demands of the curriculum and increased emphasis on formal learning, with the written word becoming more prominent as we progress through. We look at children's responses to the curriculum and reflect on how we might be able to support them through those challenges.

Chapter 5 looks at later primary school, splitting the chapter into Upper and Lower Key Stage 2. The topic of SATs in Year 6 is addressed and I look at the potential toll on children's wellbeing that can accompany SATs. Transition to secondary school is also discussed, allowing time and space to consider your own students and how you might address their challenges.

Chapter 6 looks at how dyslexia can show in secondary school, with some of the potentially problematic responses that students may have to tasks because of the challenges they experience in literacy and the curriculum more broadly. There are case studies given that show different children's and families' journeys, which provide space to reflect on their relevance to your students. As with other chapters, you are also given time and space to reflect on your own practice and any potential changes you could make.

In Chapter 7, the main stakeholders supporting a dyslexic child are discussed, and their relationship is highlighted. The team of the carers/parents, educators and the child is key; here I talk about the interplay between them and how their roles are detailed in policy across the four home nations. Case studies and reflection points provide practical strategies to help you build positive links with families and children.

In Chapter 8, we look at life after school. School is the starting point for life in some ways, and the strategies we learn there can set us up for things later on. Here I outline the importance of addressing what children and young people will do next, so that they can prepare. Traditional pathways such as university are discussed but I also showcase other avenues which children may want to pursue; there is no one model for success, and I emphasise that strongly in this chapter!

The final chapter, Chapter 9, draws together the different elements and themes of the book, to showcase how dyslexic students can flourish in the mainstream classroom; I share part of my own story. Training and professional development routes will be signposted, organisations that help families will be noted and I will also link to support organisations that empower children and young people with dyslexia.

I hope the book is useful and that you enjoy reading it!

1
Neurodiversity
A Brief History and Overview

Introduction

In this chapter, I will talk through how neurodiversity has been viewed in the past and relate dyslexia to that overview. I'll start with an overview of the social model of disability, and talk through how 'neurodiversity' fits into that understanding. Then we have a look at how dyslexia connects with neurodiversity, with brief reference to its prevalence, and then I finish with a note about how I refer to dyslexia in this book.

From a Deficit to Strength and Empowerment

During the 1960s, sociologists and psychologists like Irving Goffman explored how views of disability and differences between people influenced their engagement with society. Goffman (1963) felt that disability is linked to stigmatisation of people due to societal perceptions of them being deficient. Disability as a problem or fault with a person was linked to a medicalised understanding of disability. In a framework where disability is viewed medically, people often think of physical conditions or imagine people who use a wheelchair because these are usually identified via medical pathways. There is an oft unstated expectation that medical input will cure or improve the underlying physical problem.

Dyslexia and some other neurodiversities are not easily understood from a medical point of view; it is not possible to find them with a stethoscope and x-rays do not pick them up. While there is some research on differences in the brain of people with dyslexia when compared with those who do not have it, most people cannot access the resources needed to look at brain activity. So dyslexic people were not easy to point out in school during the mid-to-late 20th century. Their needs were often not understood;

dyslexic people (and many other neurodivergent individuals) were misunderstood as lazy, unintelligent, at times ineducable.

As psychologists and educationalists started to better understand the cognitive skills needed for different elements of literacy and numeracy development, and curricular access more generally, dyslexia and other specific learning difficulties, could be identified through educational channels. Delivery of education could be adjusted to help those with challenges in certain areas so that they can flourish (on paper at least!). The shift towards a social understanding of disability (and as part of that, neurodiversity) challenged dominant ideas around people having inherent deficiencies. Instead, people sought empowerment and to use their own voices to create their own narratives.

Neurodiversity in the Beginning

'Neurodiversity' is rooted in the social model of disability. A social model of disability does not accept that individuals have disabilities or intrinsic problems or faults. In the mid-1970s in the UK, a movement highlighting the impact of societal structures and expectations on individuals with impairments began. The Disabled People's Movement sought to highlight the disabling effect of structures/expectations, to politicise disability and create change (Disability Alliance, 1976; Hughes, 2009). The aim was to shift the discourse surrounding disability and impairment from one of medicalisation, fault within the individual and medicalised, deficit views of people, towards an empowered understanding of people, their strengths, areas of challenge and how society can adapt to make life easier for them.

Neurodiversity may feel like a term that has existed for a long time, as it is engrained in a lot of educational materials. A relatively early mention of the term was in 1997 by Judy Singer, as part of her thesis (noted in Eveleigh, 2019). In mentioning Singer and her work, I am aware that she is a controversial figure in the autism community due to her anti-trans position, as well as her views on Aspergers and use of the associated terminology. Relating to autism and her early work, Singer felt that there wasn't language existent for autistic people to describe themselves, based on both her research and experiences within her family. She believed that it was important for autistic people to have a term which did not exclude them and was empowering, rather than stigmatising. When Singer used 'neurodiversity' as a term, her main focus was on the autism community (a broader sense of neurodiversity is outlined below). Singer felt that it was important to view autistic individuals as a 'neurological minority' rather than a disabled group (Eveleigh, 2019). Over time, others have felt that this applied to other groups with the central focus of the terminology around 'neurodiversity' focussing not on 'fixing' the individual, but rather on society adapting and adjusting to be inclusive of neurodivergent individuals.

A Broader Understanding of Neurodiversity

Neurodiversity initially focussed on empowering autistic people. Recently however, the term has expanded to include conditions such as ADHD and Tourette's, as well as specific learning disabilities, such as dyslexia and dyscalculia. Although the scope of neurodiversity has broadened, the underpinning philosophy of empowerment, and embracing of the variety in people's experiences of the world around them remains. Within a social model of disability, which underpins the concept of neurodiversity, it is broadly accepted that there is no 'right' way of engaging with learning, thinking and behaving; differences are to be celebrated not viewed as problems to be rectified (Baumer and Frueh, 2021).

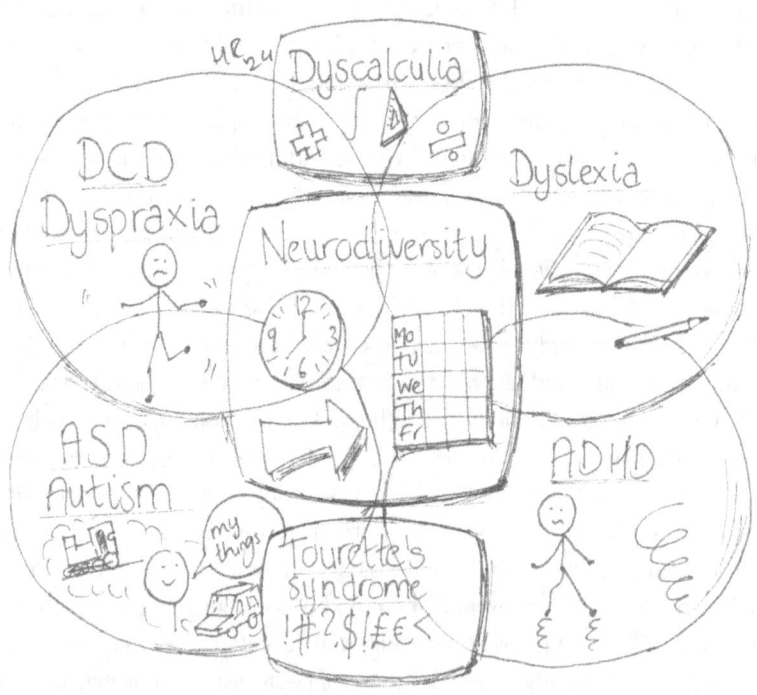

While the different conditions and ways of engaging with the world under the 'neurodiversity umbrella' do vary, there are commonalities. Often within a neurodiverse group of people, whether or not they have different diagnoses, they are likely to have vulnerabilities in their memory and organisation skills. Time management can be challenging for neurodivergent people, and organisation/concentration may not always come easily. However, this is not the case for everyone; some individuals may have strengths where others have difficulties.

As educators, we need to remember that within the different 'conditions', differences exist in how those conditions affect individuals. For example, one person with dyslexia may find reading entirely unproblematic but find spelling very difficult, whereas another dyslexic person may be able to spell and write with fluency, but find reading challenging. This is where a neurodiverse community can support and empower individuals; strengths are celebrated and challenges supported.

Dyslexia in a Neurodiverse World

I will speak about dyslexia and how it has been conceptualised historically, as well as current understandings of it in Chapter 2, so I won't go into detail to describe what dyslexia is here. However, it is important to note that the effects of dyslexia can either be exacerbated or minimised, according to how structures are organised around dyslexic people and how people respond to them. Research has noted that 'neurodiversity' now includes both educational and medical needs (Rentenbach *et al.*, 2017; den Houting, 2019). MacDonald (2019) noted that dyslexia can be supported where social accommodations are met; this is the common thread running through the 'neurodiversity' movement.

Dyslexia is a common phenomenon, affecting an estimated one in ten people (NHS, 2018) so raising awareness of it and how it can be supported is vital as we are increasingly encountering neurodivergent individuals in all spheres of life. Awareness, inclusion and supporting young people to understand their own (and others') dyslexia in a complex world will help young people as they grow to flourish and become independent adults.

Language and Terminology in this Book

Although the 'neurodiversity' movement generally works cohesively, there are some areas of difference, where different groups and individuals have different preferences. For example, classifying different conditions according to severity is not always met positively (Eveleigh, 2019). With that in mind, in this book, I will not refer to different intensities of dyslexia or different severities. I believe that we cannot discern how different people perceive their personal challenges and strengths readily as they are exactly that: personal. It is possible to refer to standardised scores arising during diagnoses or assessments, and these can help provide context. However, numbers do not operate in isolation. As we have seen above, social context can have a substantial impact on people's areas of difficulty, reducing their impact or sometimes – and very sadly – worsening it. Because of this, I will refer to people's experiences of things that work to help them and things that hinder them, rather than trying to objectively say how *bad* their dyslexia is.

As noted by Baumer and Frueh (2021), the language used to describe people and their different profiles is very important and can be a source of controversy. They observed that person-first language has been preferred by some disability organisations (eg a person with dyslexia; a person with dyscalculia). However, they also report that within the autistic community there is a preference for identity-first language (eg autistic person; dyslexic person). A different approach to terminology is apparent within the dyslexia community, with Macdonald (2019) writing 'person with dyslexia' in his work on the social model of dyslexia. This centralises the person rather than their dyslexia and is an approach used by many other researchers. However, others write about dyslexia with the label first, which aligns with the position that a label can be transformative and emancipatory for an individual. There is no agreed approach to language around dyslexia, and how it is framed when discussing individuals and their experiences. In this book, I will take a pragmatic approach to how I refer to individuals and their dyslexia (I will use identity-first language when referring to autistic people, as it is a preference within the community). I have no personal preference in how my dyslexia is described, and frequently use both person- and label-first language when I speak and write. Here, I switch between label-first and person-first language depending on the context, sentence structure and what flows best. I am dyslexic myself so I will try to make the text as accessible as possible and the language I use is part of that.

Key Takeaways

- Neurodiversity includes a range of both medical and educational needs that affect how individuals process and make sense of the world around them. It originated in the autism community as part of the community reclaiming their identity and empowering themselves.
- The 'neurodiversity' movement has many different elements but largely they agree that someone may have a medical or cognitive impairment/ difference, but that disability is a result of social structures not adapting and taking account of individuals' differences.
- Dyslexia is one of the specific learning difficulties under the 'neurodiversity' umbrella.
- The language used to describe individuals with different learning difficulties can be very controversial, sometimes dividing communities. In this book, I use both person-first and identify-first language, depending on context. I do not have personal preference as to how I am addressed or how I address myself, and my choice of phraseology in this book reflects that.

References and Further Reading

Baumer, N. and Frueh, J. (2021) 'What is neurodiversity? Harvard health'. Available at: https://www.health.harvard.edu/blog/what-is-neurodiversity-202111232645 (Accessed: 18 August 2023).

Disability Alliance (1976) *Fundamental Principles of Disability*. London: UPIAS and The Disability Alliance.

Eveleigh, A. (2019) 'The origins and evolution of neurodiversity, neurodiversity media'. Available at: https://www.neurodiversitymedia.com/resource-library/the-origins-and-evolution-of-neurodiversity (Accessed: 18 August 2023).

Goffman, E. (1963) *Stigma: Notes on the Management of Spoiled Identity*. London: Penguin.

den Houting, J. (2019) 'Neurodiversity: An insider's perspective', *Autism*, 23(2), pp. 271–273. https://doi.org/10.1177/1362361318820762.

Hughes, B. (2009) 'Disability activisms: Social model stalwarts and biological citizens', *Disability & Society*, 24(6), pp. 677–688. https://doi.org/10.1080/09687590903160118.

Macdonald, S. (2019) 'From "disordered" to "diverse": Defining six sociological frameworks employed in the study of Dyslexia in the UK'. *Insights on Learning Disabilities*, 16(1), pp. 1–22.

NHS (2018) 'Dyslexia, nhs.uk'. Available at: https://www.nhs.uk/conditions/dyslexia/ (Accessed: 16 September 2022).

Rentenbach, B., Prislovsky, L. and Gabriel, R. (2017) 'Valuing differences: Neurodiversity in the classroom'. *Phi Delta Kappan*, 98(8), pp. 59–63. https://doi.org/10.1177/0031721717708297.

2
Dyslexia
More Than Just a Reading Problem

Introduction

Dyslexia is a contested phenomenon and there is no unified definition of it, despite it having been studied for hundreds of years (Frith, 1999). The underlying causes are becoming more widely agreed upon (World Health Organisation, 2023; Carroll et al., 2024; Holden et al., 2024) and linked to definitions which can be used by clinicians and practitioners; this is discussed in this chapter, with a brief overview of some history of dyslexia and its 'predecessors'. However, the existence of dyslexia is not universally agreed. *The Dyslexia Debate* (Elliott and Grigorenko, 2014) sparked a lot of interest with its critique of dyslexia and whether it should be viewed as a separate category of reading difficulty, or whether it should be included in more general reading challenges. This is not discussed in detail here, but it is an interesting position and worth exploring if you are interested. This chapter focusses on definitions of dyslexia and how they are used in practice, with detailed definitions that are drawn on globally and in the UK.

Foundations of 'Dyslexia'

For me, the concept of being 'well read' is connected to perceptions of how clever someone is. So if someone *isn't* well read, they can be seen as not bright, less engaged with the world around them and as having less potential. This is really problematic, because it looks to only one, very limited, traditionally academic view of 'clever' and even then, it doesn't do traditionally academically able people justice. Not everyone likes to read. Not everyone focusses on reading and not everyone who reads is academically inclined. However, some roots of dyslexia do link back to literacy generally, and whether or how well people can read. This section gives a brief overview of how dyslexia has been framed and how understandings have changed since 'word blindness' was conceived.

> **❓ Reflection Point: What Do You Think Dyslexia Is?**
>
> You have picked up this book because you have an interest in dyslexia and are motivated to find out more. Different people picking up this book will have different starting points, so it's really important to start from where *you* are and develop your understanding rather than focussing on others and their journeys. At this point, stop and think (you might want to make notes on this or not – it is entirely up to you!):
>
> - What do you know about dyslexia?
> - What does it affect?
> - How do you know that it is there?

Word Blindness and Dyslexia

Despite some viewing reading as a reflection of intelligence, there has been substantial research into why people who seem to be bright and generally able may struggle to read (Shaywitz, 2005). In the 17th century, the phrase 'word blindness' was coined by Johannes Schmidt. He was a linguist and his account of an individual unable to read is the first instance where reading difficulties were attributed to cognitive rather than optical difficulties (Kirby and Snowling, 2022). However, despite Schmidt addressing non-optical reading challenges, it was not until the 19th century that 'dyslexia' was used as a phrase by Rudolf Berlin, an ophthalmologist in Stuttgart (Kirby, 2018). He used the term to mean 'difficulties' with words (Kirby and Snowling, 2022) and this tends to be how dyslexia is viewed nowadays.

Towards 'Modern' Views

There is a lot of history to explore around dyslexia in the world and I have put a few sources in the Key Takeaways section of this chapter so you can have a look if you want to. I'm skipping over much of the 20th century and how dyslexia started to be conceptualised. In the 1970s, research started to look at how language and reading development were connected. Leong (1978) linked dyslexia to challenges in phonological processing but this was still a fairly limited view of what can impede reading. Towards the end of the 20th century, Calfee (1983: 7) broadened the concept of dyslexia to the failure of apparently normal youngsters to become skilled readers after instruction which was apparently effective for their peers. While this was helpful in some ways, it was not necessarily usefully defined for assessors/ psychologists, because underlying causes were not suggested in this view. However, moving towards the 21st century, definitions were developed that started to unify both underlying causes and measurable academic outcomes. The Rose Report (Rose, 2009) was a seminal report written as part of a call for evidence in 2008[1] and constructed a working definition of dyslexia that underpins the recent definitions used by the British Dyslexia Association (BDA, 2010) inter alia- see below.

---

1   The original call for evidence website address is given on page 1 of the Rose Report but it is not currently accessible http://www.dcsf.gov.uk/pns/DisplayPN.cgi?pn_id=2008_0148 (access sought 8 January 2024).

'Dyslexias' Today

In this section, some different English-language definitions of dyslexia are discussed. It is important to note that there is no single definition of dyslexia globally. Other languages frame dyslexia differently, as it can manifest differently depending on the characteristics of a language and the cultural context. The definitions here are ordered so that they are more general in their description. They then move towards a definition which is often used for diagnostic and training purposes in England and elsewhere. At the time of writing, this definition was in pre-print and under peer review, although it is being used by assessors at the recommendation of SASC (SASC, 2024), which is our professional overseeing body as Specialist Assessors.

International Classification of Diseases (ICD)

The International Classification of Diseases from the World Health Organisation has recently updated its description of specific learning difficulties. The overview notes that there may be 'persistent difficulties in learning academic skills, which may include reading, writing or arithmetic' (World Health Organisation, 2023), with an individual's academic attainment being lower than others their age. Underpinning clinical features of these challenges are noted as being

> impairments in phonological processing, orthographic processing, memory (including working memory), executive functions (including inhibitory control, set-shifting, planning), learning and automatizing symbols (e.g., visual, alphanumeric), perceptual-motor integration, and speed of processing information.
>
> (ibid)

This provides an overview for all specific learning difficulties rather than literacy independently.

British Psychological Society

Crombie, writing in 2022, posited that dyslexia needed to be redefined. Part of her reasoning for this was that assessing for dyslexia was complicated by the way dyslexia is operationalised. She felt that framing it within a deficit-model locates the problem within the child. At the time of her writing, the definition of dyslexia employed by the British Psychological Society (BPS, 1999) did not include reference to the underpinning cognitive processing challenges linked to it:

> Dyslexia is evident when accurate and fluent word reading and/ or spelling develops very incompletely or with great difficulty. This focuses on literacy learning at the 'word level' (reading a word with no cues from any context in a sentence, no pictures, etc.) and implies that the problem is severe and persistent despite appropriate learning opportunities. It provides the basis for a staged process of assessment through teaching.

While this definition does note that there are challenges with word-level reading and spelling, the underlying mechanisms and challenges are not referred to, which does make definitive assessment of dyslexia challenging within this framework.

British Dyslexia Association

The definition of dyslexia adopted by the British Dyslexia Association builds on the Rose (2009) definition but also considers coordination, calculation, elements of executive function and personal organisation challenges. This connects effectively with the current ICD 11 (World Health Organisation, 2023) definition, as well as the ICD 10 conceptualisation of literacy challenges (World Health Organisation, 2016). The definition is as follows (BDA, 2010):

> Dyslexia is a learning difficulty that primarily affects the skills involved in accurate and fluent word reading and spelling. Characteristic features of dyslexia are difficulties in phonological awareness, verbal memory and verbal processing speed. Dyslexia occurs across the range of intellectual abilities. It is best thought of as a continuum, not a distinct category, and there are no clear cut-off points. Co-occurring difficulties may be seen in aspects of language, motor co-ordination, mental calculation, concentration and personal organisation, but these are not, by themselves, markers of dyslexia. A good indication of the severity and persistence of dyslexic difficulties can be gained by examining how the individual responds or has responded to well-founded intervention.

Within this conceptualisation, as with the ICD 11 (World Health Organisation, 2023) view, underpinning cognitive processes are clearly noted, which allows them to be assessed and monitored. In addition to the challenges experienced by dyslexic individuals, the BDA (2010) definition also highlights some strengths that they may have, drawing on 'areas, such as design, problem solving, creative skills, interactive skills and oral skills. This starts to move towards an empowerment model of dyslexia, rather than purely deficit model, as suggested by Crombie, (2022).

SASC and the Delphi Study

In May 2024, findings were published from a three-year long study led by a cross-section of academics, and informed by views from various professionals such as Specialist Assessors, Educational Psychologists, university support practitioners and other academics (Carroll et al., 2024; Holden et al., 2024). The study was designed to garner views from different stakeholders in the dyslexia community and push for consensus in developing a conceptualisation of dyslexia. At the time of writing, papers relating to the study are under review but can be read in pre-print form; the review time frame is at present unknown. There has been a briefing released with official guidance relating to the study from SASC in which the definition arising from the study is summarised: (SASC, 2024)

Nature
The nature and developmental trajectory of dyslexia depends on multiple genetic and environmental influences.

Manifestation
Dyslexia is a set of processing difficulties that affect the acquisition of reading and spelling. The most commonly observed cognitive impairment in dyslexia is a difficulty in phonological processing (i.e. in phonological awareness, phonological processing speed or phonological memory). However, phonological difficulties do not fully explain the variability that is observed. Working memory, processing speed and orthographic skills can contribute to the impact of dyslexia.

Impact
In dyslexia, some or all aspects of literacy attainment are weak in relation to age, standard teaching and instruction, and level of other attainments. Across languages and age groups, difficulties in reading and spelling fluency are a key marker of dyslexia.

Variance and co-occurrence
Dyslexic difficulties exist on a continuum and can be experienced to various degrees of severity. Dyslexia can affect the acquisition of other skills, such as mathematics, reading comprehension or learning another language. Dyslexia frequently co-occurs with one or more other developmental difficulties, including developmental language disorder, dyscalculia, ADHD, and developmental coordination disorder.

Like many other definitions, this definition links to phonological processing, which includes phonological awareness and memory (these are separately considered by Rose, 2009), as well as working memory and processing speed. In addition, orthographic skills are included here, which links to writing, spelling and penmanship more generally. The main difference between this definition and others is that the impact of the manifestation is explicitly noted, which does map onto current understandings of disability with legislation and the effect of impairment/disability in defining disability (HMSO, 2010). This definition also explicitly acknowledges the prevalence of co-occurring difficulties alongside dyslexia; this was alluded to by Rose (2009) and in the British Dyslexia Association (BDA, 2010) but particular categories of challenge were not identified. It is also helpful for those who do not work in the 'field' of dyslexia to understand the underlying and varying cognitive challenges that individuals may have, and how those challenges map onto vulnerabilities in attainment; these are clearly outlined within this definition. Although the papers are not formally published, SASC does not envisage that substantive changes will be expected during the publication process of the review and information on this will be available on the SASC website, details of which are given below.

> ### ? Reflection Point: What Do You Think Dyslexia Is?
>
> We are circling back to the initial question and thought process from this chapter. I asked you at the start to consider the following questions:
>
> - What do you know about dyslexia?
> - What does it affect?
> - How do you know that it is there?
>
> Now you have had the chance to have a look through different understandings and conceptualisations of dyslexia, have your thoughts changed? Are there commonalities across the definitions? Are there substantive differences between them that do not seem to align at all? What is your take on any of those differences?
>
> Remember that there are no right or wrong answers to this set of questions. There are your views and they are the ones that matter, and how you view dyslexia may evolve over time or as you work with different individuals and/or groups of people

Concluding Remarks: Definition Choice and Implications

Different practitioners in the English-context are bound by different professional expectations and codes of practice. I am a Specialist Assessor of dyslexia, dyscalculia and specific learning difficulties. There is an overview of different definitions of dyslexia used in the UK in the Key Takeaways section of this chapter, which gives some insight into how it is operationalised for professionals. At the time of writing, my professional membership and registration is with the British Dyslexia Association; it has been with them since I qualified in 2020. This does inform the definition that I used in my assessments: I use the BDA definition (2010) at the time of writing this but I will now be moving forwards to using the finalised Delphi definition in due course, if that is expected professionally. Importantly, both definitions do link to phonological processing (awareness and memory), verbal processing and verbal memory, and note the vulnerability of weaknesses in these areas to impact attainment in literacy and other areas. The BDA definition (2010) (alongside the others used in the UK) has clear concepts that can be measured, whether informally by educators to monitor progress, or formally as part of assessment processes. The underlying cognitive processes linked to dyslexia are noted, as well as academic areas of achievement which can be tested, both to monitor progress and as part of assessment. There are other definitions that I have described, which also have strengths and are used by other professionals. From a pragmatic perspective, the key thing to be aware of when looking to understand dyslexia from the perspective of young people is to read through assessment reports and see how the writer has linked the student's profile to the definition, and then used that connection to explain how young people learn and why certain elements of literacy and learning may be tricky for them.

Reflection Point: What Thoughts Have Been Challenged?

Hopefully this short-ish chapter has given you some insight into how people first became aware of dyslexia, its evolution as a concept and where it sits within current educational frameworks. Reflect for a moment:

- What didn't you know before and how is your new insight useful?
- What did you know and how is that confirmation helpful?
- What insight did the case study give you from the perspective of an individual who is not an educator and how can you use that in your teaching?

Key Takeaways

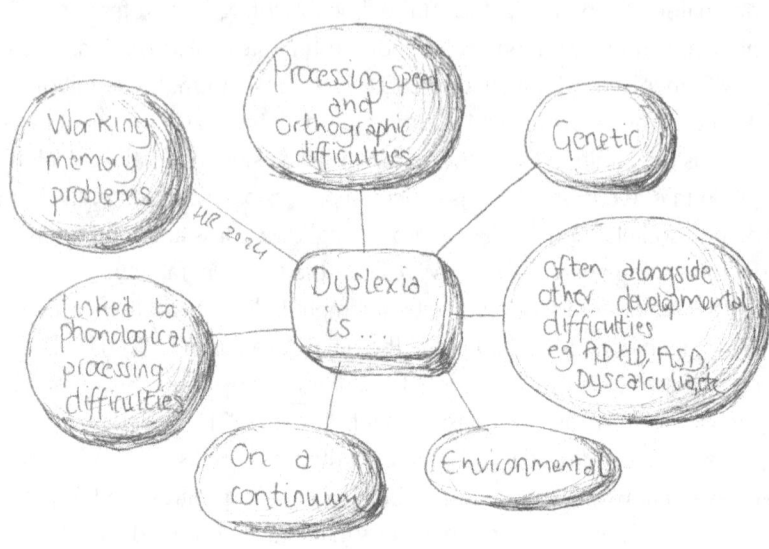

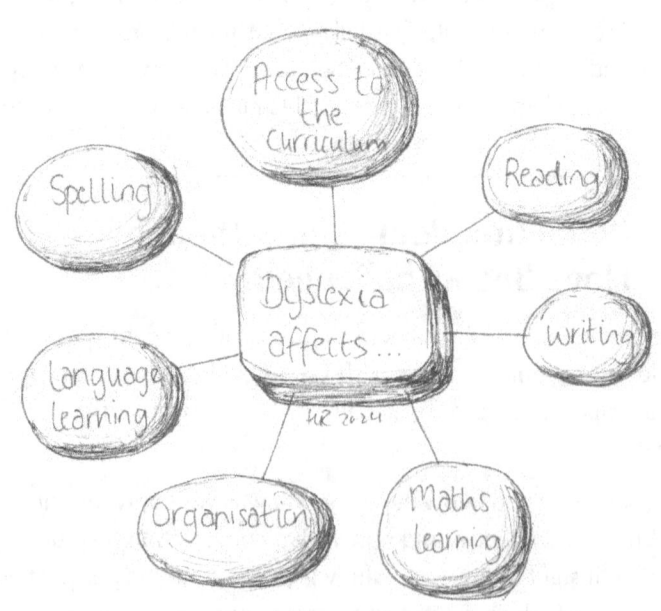

- Dyslexia has long been a 'disorder' that is not fully accepted with definitions of it varying across language and culture, and even within the same country. At present, generally it is accepted in the Anglophone world as being linked to challenges in phonological processing, verbal memory, processing speed and orthographic skills.
- Dyslexia tends to impact most 'obviously' on reading fluency but can also affect spelling, writing, reading comprehension and due to the challenges in working memory, other areas such as maths may be negatively affected.
- Dyslexia often co-occurs with other neurodiversities and unpicking the impact of those different challenges can be tricky; a multiprofessional team may be implicated in doing so.
- Early identification of dyslexia is important.

Further Reading

- The Specific Learning Difficulties Assessment Standards Committee updates guidance relating to dyslexia, dyscalculia and assessment regularly. They will share information about the Delphi study and any subsequent implications of that paper in due course. Information can be found on their website, in the 'news' section. The link to their website is here: https://sasc.org.uk/.
- In Scotland, practice and policy relating to special educational needs differs substantially from the other regions of the UK. Dyslexia Scotland has a comprehensive and insightful definition of dyslexia. The definition generally aligns with other views of dyslexia, but also explicitly considers the impact in relation to learning and teaching settings. You can see the definition here: https://dyslexiascotland.org.uk/what-is-dyslexia/
- This definition is also cited by the Northern Ireland Dyslexia Centre on their website, which also gives helpful insight into how dyslexia can show in day-to-day life: https://www.nidyslexiacentre.co.uk/what-is-dyslexia/
- In Wales, there is support available in both Welsh and English from Dyslecsia Cymru/Wales Dyslexia. They offer support for

practitioners as well as those with dyslexia. Their website is available here: https://www.walesdyslexia.org.uk/
- The International Dyslexia Association, which largely operates in North America, has a definition of dyslexia that links to challenges in phonological skills and can be seen here: https://dyslexiaida.org/definition-of-dyslexia/
- The Australian Dyslexia Association does not define dyslexia in a short few paragraphs, as is done by the other sources cited here. Instead, their website gives an overview of how it may appear and what primary challenges are linked to dyslexia. Although they do link to phonological awareness challenges, other underlying cognitive skills are not mentioned here: https://dyslexiaassociation.org.au/what-is-dyslexia/.
- Dr Martin Bloomfield has been working on a project where dyslexia definitions and assessments across Europe have been explored, summarised and collated. You can explore the Dyslexia Compass here: https://dyslexiacompass.eu/.
- For historical understandings of dyslexia you can look at the British Psychological Society website here https://www.bps.org.uk/psychologist/brief-history-dyslexia, or you may find the US-based National Library of Medicine link to a book by Dr Philip Kirby and Professor Margaret J. Snowling useful here: https://www.ncbi.nlm.nih.gov/books/NBK588803/#:~:text=In%201676%2C%20a%20German%20linguist,read%20for%20non%2Doptical%20reasons.
- You can watch a video about the history of dyslexia here: https://youtu.be/uMN7jL2m0Js?si=n2qrUDn_PoZmJobi. The video was produced by Succeed with Dyslexia and is hosted by Darren Clark. It is freely available on YouTube.

References and Bibliography

British Dyslexia Association (BDA) (2010) *What Is Dyslexia?* British Dyslexia Association. Available at: https://www.bdadyslexia.org.uk/dyslexia/about-dyslexia/what-is-dyslexia (Accessed: 21 July 2022).

British Psychological Society (BPS) (1999) *A Framework for Psychological Assessment and Intervention*. DECP Newsletter February 1999. Leicester: British Psychological Society.

Calfee, R. (1983) 'The mind of the dyslexic'. *Annals of Dyslexia*, 33, pp. 9–28. Available at: https://doi.org/10.1007/BF02647993.

Carroll, J. et al. (2024) 'Contemporary concepts of dyslexia: A Delphi study'. Available at: https://osf.io/preprints/osf/tb8mp.

Crombie, M. (2022) 'Redefining dyslexia, British psychological society'. Available at: https://www.bps.org.uk/psychologist/redefining-dyslexia (Accessed: 8 January 2024).

Elliott, J. and Grigorenko, E. L. (2014) *The Dyslexia Debate*. 1st ed. Cambridge: Cambridge : Cambridge University Press.

Frith, U. (1999) 'Paradoxes in the definition of Dyslexia'. *Dyslexia*, 5, pp. 192–214

HMSO (2010) *Equality Act 2010*. Statute Law Database. Available at: https://www.legislation.gov.uk/ukpga/2010/15/contents (Accessed: 15 February 2022).

Holden, C. et al. (2024) 'Towards a consensus for dyslexia practice: Findings of a Delphi study on assessment and identification'. Available at: https://osf.io/preprints/edarxiv/g7m8n.

Kirby, P. (2018) 'A brief history of dyslexia, BPS'. Available at: https://www.bps.org.uk/psychologist/brief-history-dyslexia (Accessed: 8 January 2024).

Kirby, P. and Snowling, M.J. (2022) 'Dyslexia discovered: Word-blindness, Victorian medicine, and education (1877–1917)'. In *Dyslexia: A History [Internet]*. McGill-Queen's University Press. Available at: https://www.ncbi.nlm.nih.gov/books/NBK588803/ (Accessed: 8 January 2024).

Leong, C.K. (1978) 'Children's concepts of language in learning to read'. *Bulletin of the Orton Society*, 29(1), pp. 114–128.

Rose, J. (2009) 'Identifying and teaching children and young people with Dyslexia and literacy difficulties an independent report from Sir Jim Rose to the secretary of stage for children, schools and families'. *DCSF* [Preprint]. Available at: http://www.thedyslexia-spldtrust.org.uk/media/downloads/inline/the-rose-report.1294933674.pdf (Accessed: 9 December 2022).

Shaywitz, S.E. (2005) *Overcoming Dyslexia*. New York: Alfred Knopf.

Specific Learning Difficulties Assessment Standards Committee (SASC) (2024) *Briefing Paper: SASC and the Delphi Dyslexia Study 2024*, p. 3. Available at: https://sasc.org.uk/media/3imfgx54/sasc-briefing-paper-delphi-dyslexia-study-may-2024-final.pdf (Accessed: 13 June 2024).

Literacy Learning Journeys

World Health Organisation (2016) 'ICD-10 Version:2016'. Available at: https://icd.who.int/browse10/2016/en#F81.1 (Accessed: 20 April 2023).

World Health Organisation (2023) 'ICD-11 for mortality and morbidity statistics, 6A03 developmental learning disorder'. Available at: https://icd.who.int/browse11/l-m/en#/http%3a%2f%2fid.who.int%2ficd%2fentity%2f2099676649 (Accessed: 8 January 2024).

3
Dyslexia in the Early Years

Introduction

Dyslexia in the Early Years can seem somewhat nebulous. Young children do not write or read much until Reception Class, so the classic 'symptoms' of dyslexia may not show. However, there are many ways that dyslexia can be apparent during the Early Years. This chapter explores this, referring to children's expected development during this phase. Before diving into the chapter, I will be explicitly clear about what I mean by Early Years. Within the English education system the phase is defined as, 'from birth to 5 years old' (UK Government, Undated). If young children attend a pre-school setting, their progress is tracked against developmental goals for each of the substages within the Early Years phase (DfE, 2023). Where children do not attend a pre-school setting, families will be supported in tracking their children's progress by local teams of Health Visitors, who monitor seven different areas of development.

Towards the end of the chapter, you will have a chance to reflect on your own understanding and practice through some short reflection activities. If you want to explore any of the ideas shared here, further reading and resources are signposted for you at the end of the chapter. Broadly this chapter covers:

- The connection between literacy development and speech/language.
- Challenges in speech sounds and phonological awareness are discussed as potential signs of literacy difficulty.
- The complexity of the spelling system in English is discussed and the potential challenges it can pose in the Early Years.
- Practical examples are given of how dyslexia may appear in young children, and strategies to support them are also given.

Literacy Learning Journeys

> **? Reflection Point: What do We Know about the Early Years?**
>
> Not everyone who works with children and young people has a full understanding of what 'happens' in the Early Years. My training as a secondary teacher covered bits about primary school, particularly Upper Key Stage 2, but nothing about the Early Years. The Early Years are sometimes overlooked, and their importance not wholly appreciated.
>
> Here, before you read and work through this chapter, take a moment to reflect on what you think are the most important developmental steps during the Early Years. These may be social, academic and/or physical.
>
> There are no right or wrong answers.
> There are your answers, based on your journey, your experiences and your understanding of the world.
>
> You may find it helpful to make a note of your thoughts as you go along. Sometimes it can be really good to see how thoughts and preconceptions change (or not!) as we work through different processes!

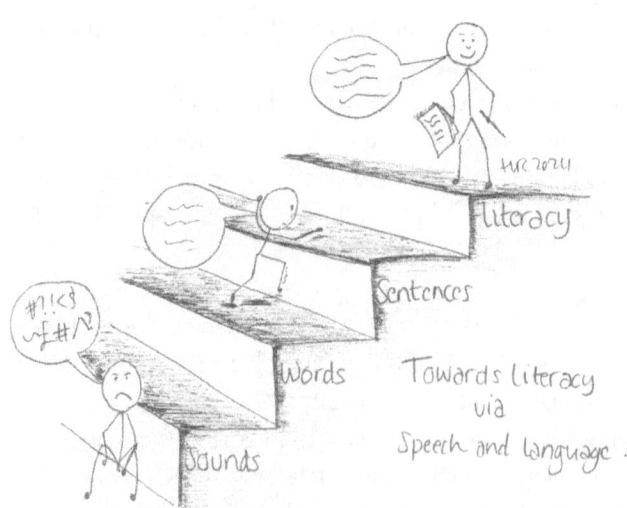

Towards Literacy via Speech and language.

Language and Communication: the Early Years

In this section, we will think about language and communication development across the Early Years. We will start at the point of language sounds and word formation, and look at their evolution into words, then full speech. The chapter does not delve, full-speed into the realm of speech and language but gives an overview of how speech and language link to literacy development. With practicality, and looking forward onto the next phase of education (Key Stage 1), this section will finish by outlining the language and communication skills that young people are expected to have, and will need, as they start Key Stage 1.

Where Do Young People Start: 0–3

When they are very young, babies and toddlers don't usually use full sentences and words but they do start to recognise sounds very quickly. Within the Development Matters guidance (DfE, 2023), it is expected that babies will turn to face sounds they recognise, and – right from an early age – will copy how the adults around them take turns in speech. Babies even try to mimic lip movements! As they progress towards pre-school age, babies and toddlers use sounds to communicate what they want to do, to express their feelings and sometimes just to get attention. Children really are amazing and everything they do, even babbling and making noises as they play, is a learning process; these noises are a precursor to speech.

Children's listening develops so they can understand others and make sense of what is happening around them. Moving through from being babies, towards toddler-hood, and listening to others helps the development of children's speech sounds such as /p/, /b/, /m/ and /w/ (DfE, 2023). They use these sounds to form words and move towards making sentences. However, if they cannot make sounds or words so that others can understand, it can be frustrating for children and interacting with others may be difficult.

What Happens Along the Way: 3–4

Between the ages of three and four, children's speech and language goes through substantial development. Their knowledge of words will broaden and they will then work with complex sentences as part of instructions or discussions (DfE, 2023). Nursery rhymes, songs and stories start to figure in their interactions, with children singing or saying rhymes, and telling stories they have heard. Children start to speak in sentences of 4–6 words (DfE, 2023) and start to share their views in more detail. They may share their agreement or disagreement with others and start multi-turn conversations.

The speech sounds that children make become more complex and children will usually begin to say multisyllabic words. Although they may not always use verbal tenses and pluralised words as expected, young people will start to try using them, and largely these will be comprehensible, as they are based on patterns that children have recognised from other sources. Sounds children use are more complex and rely on the solid foundations developed when the children were younger. If basic speech sounds are not secure, then more complex ones are at risk of not developing as expected, which can impact on language/communication skills, potentially negatively impacting on children's learning as they approach school and Key Stage 1.

Approaching Key Stage 1 and Beyond: 5 and Upwards

By the time children are in Reception Class, their speech and language is expected to be such that they can express themselves in complex sentences, link ideas and give detail in their explanations of events and stories. Children's vocabulary knowledge expands substantially during Reception Year so they can use their talk to work out problems and organise their thinking. Sharing information and working with others is part of this; children are expected to develop their interaction skills through working with and talking with others. Learning rhymes and songs continues to be an area of activity for children, where they are also expected to concentrate on the sounds of the songs as they learn them. Children's vocabulary knowledge is part of their toolkit to help them make sense of the world around them.

Interestingly, within the Development Matters framework (DfE, 2023) for children in Reception Year, allowances for areas of challenge do not appear to be made. It appears that speech sounds are all expected to be in place for all children by the time they complete their Early Years phase. No explicit consideration is given to children who have not mastered those skills. This can have serious implications for those children, as difficulties in speech sounds link to challenges in reading and also dyslexia (Cabbage et al., 2018).

Reflection Point: Speech and Language Knowledge

Children's speech and language development is a crucial part of the Early Years journey, and if they have challenges here it can have substantial and often negative impacts on their broader development. While speech and language do develop 'naturally' for most children, some children find it difficult to make themselves understood. Even where this is not the case, parents, teachers and other adults in those children's lives can hugely impact on how their speech develops. At this point, I would like you to think about what you might be able to do to support speech/language development for children in your setting.

Children's capabilities and development vary across the Early Years, so you may find it helpful to look at Development Matters (DfE, 2023) as a reference point when considering the following questions:

- What can they do?
- Are there any sounds or words that they find tricky?
- Are there any known difficulties with language experienced by other members of their family?
- What do they need to be able to do?
- What am I good at and what is my role with this child?
- How can I use those skills in a setting where we operate to help them reach their goals?

Speech for Literacy: Why Language Matters

Language development and literacy are inextricably linked. To be able to make sense of the written word, children need to be able to articulate and manipulate the sounds linked to the written representation of those sounds. In this section, I discuss how difficulties in engaging with speech sounds (often known as phonemes when referring to literacy development) can manifest in the Early Years, as well as their roots in phonological vulnerabilities. The opacity of the English-language spelling system is also considered and the challenges relating to complex spelling systems are explored (Herrington and Macken-Horarik, 2015).

Speech Sounds in Literacy

For most of the Early Years, literacy is grounded in speech and language. From 0–3, books and stories are shared, but young people are not expected to read. They are read to, sounds are focussed on, rhymes and songs are a source of learning, and printed letters are only introduced with a light touch (DfE, 2023). As young people reach 3–4 years old, they become familiar

Dyslexia in the Early Years

with concepts linked to the written word and understand that print conveys meaning and has many different purposes. The direction of reading (left to right) is introduced, and books may be discussed in more detail.

At this point, purposeful and active development of children's phonological awareness really takes off. The rhyming and sound games that young people have likely engaged in become more complex, with rhythm, syllable counting and comparison of sounds taking place. If young people have experienced challenges in developing those speech sounds, this stage of literacy development can be very problematic. Herrington and Macken-Horarik (2015) found overlap between children with dyslexia and speech/language difficulties, which showed through their processing of sound. In younger children, if they do not discern sounds as expected, they may not perceive similarities or differences between words. This can impact on spelling or reading later on, amplified by the complexity of the English spelling system.

Sounds and Letters: the Opacity of English

English has a complex spelling system, where letters and sounds do not always directly map onto each other as might be expected (and sometimes hoped!). Languages with complex spelling systems can be known as 'opaque'

37

systems, and a lot of work has been done about how literacy development differs across opaque languages (like English), versus transparent ones (like Spanish or Italian), where letters do directly and consistently map onto specific sounds. Work done by Borleffs *et al*. (2019) found that developing literacy skills is more challenging in languages where sounds do not directly map on to letters and there are many different ways to make the same sound.

So, where young people find speech sounds difficult, literacy acquisition in English can be really hard!

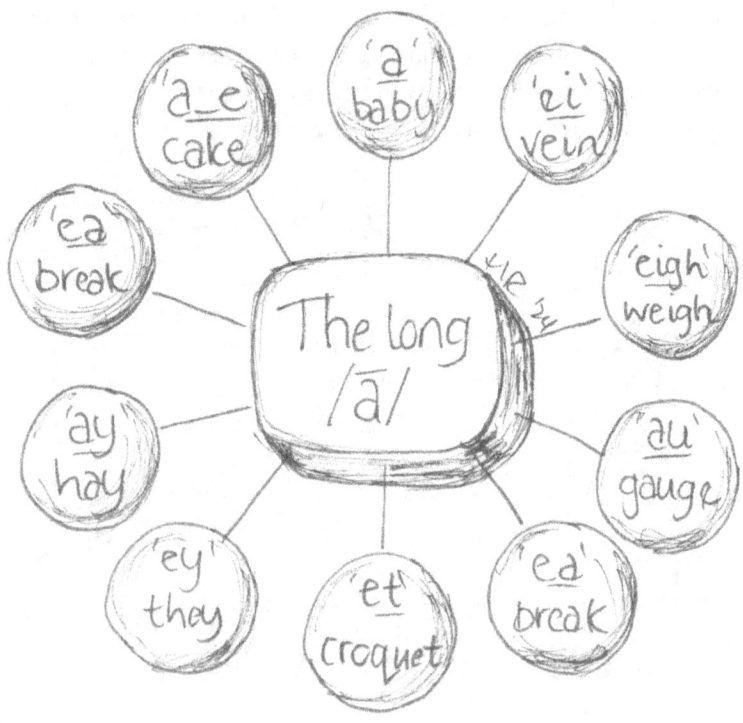

As we have seen in work by Herrington and Macken-Horarik (2015), where children have vulnerabilities in their speech and language development, difficulties with phonological awareness may co-occur. Challenges in differentiating sounds may mean that children cannot readily link sounds to letters, a skill worked on in Reception Class in England. Such challenges seen early and alongside other vulnerabilities/areas of difficulty may be an early indicator of dyslexia.

> **? Reflection Point: the Bonkersness of English!**
>
> English is a complex language. The spelling and writing system is neither wholly phonological nor morphological. Sadly, for those of us who do find spelling and reading tricky, English seems to be an inharmonious mixture of sounds and shapes (Herrington and Macken-Horarik, 2015). The phonological bits never seem to quite follow the rules and the morphological bits don't always do what you think they should! This exercise will demonstrate how complex spelling rules and systems can impact on the written word.
>
> The phrase below is a well-known saying and is wholly written using phonologically plausible letter combinations. However, it is not written as expected so it is tricky to decode. For children who have dyslexia or more general literacy difficulties, linking letters to sounds can be very difficult and it is made worse by the inconsistencies in English.
>
> **Bewty's en th' ah-ee ov th'beehowld-uh**
>
> Spend time now trying to write this phrase in 'incorrect' but plausible ways! See if you can come up with three or four alternatives.
>
> Young people who find speech sounds tricky are likely to find letter sounds and mapping them to symbols tricky. This can mean they know the rules but just don't apply them as you might expect. This pattern can start as early as Reception Year.

Where the Disjoint Starts: How Can We See Dyslexia in the Early Years

Dyslexia is often viewed as a deficit in children's (and adults') ability to work with and make sense of verbal information. The definition was explored in the last chapter, so you are already familiar with how it is currently conceptualised. Often we hear about – and I myself refer to this in my assessment reports – a discrepancy between written and spoken outputs. Children in the Early Years do not tend to produce extended pieces of writing but they are starting to engage with the written word, letters and manipulation of language. These elements and others are explored here, alongside a case study of a child who was finding literacy tricky. Strategies used to support her with her literacy are shared as part of this.

Spoken Word

We have seen already that there may be overlap between children with difficulties in their speech sounds and those with vulnerability in their phonological awareness (Herrington and Macken-Horarik, 2015). However, this does not necessarily give a practical sense of what that means in a classroom setting. I will give a brief overview here, drawing from my professional experiences, and from the interviews and discussions I had as I researched this book.

Mixing Sounds

When children are learning to speak and manipulate sounds, part of that journey often involves making mistakes, which is acknowledged within the Communication and Language frameworks, particularly for those ages 0–3 (DfE, 2023). They may find it tricky to discern between /th/, /v/ and /f/, which can have implications for children even as they are saying, then writing words such as 'van', 'fan' and 'than'. Other sounds that can be conflated are /d/, /j/ and /t/, which may make it tricky for children when they write 'dump', or 'jump', which can be sometimes seen written 'tump'.

Rhyme and Similarity

Hearing where words are the same can be a very helpful strategy for young people when they are broadening their vocabulary, and starting to try to make sense of groups of sounds. Discerning where words rhyme or sound similar, and being able to explain why, is important as children develop their literacy skills. Challenges here can make spelling similar sounding words tricky and impede fluency of spelling; each word will be treated separately rather than linked to other words. This shows even with words such as 'can,' 'ban,' 'man,' etc., for some children.

Letters and Sounds

In English, many sounds do not map directly onto one letter or a group of letters consistently, which can be challenging when engaging with the written word. Although much work with letters and sounds is done verbally and aurally in the Early Years, as they progress from four years old and move into Reception Year, children are expected to start to recognise letters. In Reception Year, children are expected to recognise sounds linked to individual letters, and move on towards recognising groups of letters and linking them to sounds.

If children find it tricky to make or discern different sounds, they may have difficulty linking those sounds to the expected letters. Although in the Early Years, the immediate impact of this is relatively small, as children progress through school they may have challenges in their spelling and reading development, if areas of vulnerability are not addressed. As is so often noted in the Special Educational Needs and Disability Code of Practice (DfE and DfH, 2015), early identification of needs is essential so that young people are supported appropriately and their needs addressed.

Sequences and Patterns

Working memory is an area of challenge for people with dyslexia (Daneman and Merikle, 1996; Schwering and MacDonald, 2020). For older children with dyslexia, vulnerabilities in their verbal working memory can show through their written outputs: work may seem disorganised or young people cannot produce as much as their peers. Reading comprehension and spelling difficulties also link to challenges in working memory, alongside problems in self-organisation.

In the Early Years, challenges in working memory show differently. Working with sequences such as days of the week, months of the year, and even seasons can be tricky if young people's verbal memory has vulnerabilities. It can also be difficult for them to recall instructions and lists. Daily routines can be also tricky for children to pick up. Difficulties in remembering song words and stories can also highlight memory difficulties; it can also be very upsetting for children when they can't do or remember things other children can. Working memory difficulties and sequences can also make it tricky for children explain events and timelines in their own lives; again this can be upsetting and frustrating for them.

Sense-making and Time-taking

Making sense of the world and filing information in and out of your mind can be a really tricky process for some people, while others just seem to 'get it' easily. This difference in individuals' sense-making can be seen from very early on; verbal processing starts as soon as babies are born and people talk to them!

Verbal processing can be defined as, 'the ability to encode, store, and manipulate linguistic information in working memory' (Daneman and Merikle, 1996), and where children have weaknesses in this skill, they need just a bit longer to process information. Children may seem like they're not listening, or may click into action a moment after others when doing a task. They may be a little slower when talking or expressing themselves because they need time to think of what to say or to find a particular word. Again, this can be perceptible to children and their peers, and can be frustrating for them.

Name and role: Stephanie started her teaching career as a secondary teacher but before that she had worked in advertising, so she was used to working with the written word and enjoyed working with language. She did mainly supply teaching when she first qualified and spent a lot of time in Early Years classrooms. After spending a lot of time in those settings and running a nursery, Stephanie decided that she would qualify as a specialist dyslexia teacher, and now works in that capacity.

Who was having a difficult time? Stephanie's daughter Lilah had a tricky time in pre-school when her group was introduced to the written word. She found it very tricky to engage and seemed to find Wednesdays at nursery very difficult. After some reflection, Stephanie worked out that Wednesday was literacy day, where the children spent a lot of time working on their letters. Lilah did not enjoy working with letters and actively avoided it where she could. Lilah was later found to be dyslexic.

What was happening? Lilah usually went in full-effort, full-speed and thoroughly enjoyed everything she did in her pre-school. Stephanie said that Lilah was always first into everything and had a real zest for everything she did but this was not the case for letters. Lilah had no interest in working with letters, finding phonics very difficult to remember. Stephanie said that phonics did not make sense to Lilah as a way of breaking down words, particularly when they were taught through very traditional methods.

What did she do about it? Stephanie used her own training in literacy as a dyslexia specialist and supported Lilah herself. She used multi-sensory strategies to help Lilah link letters to sounds. Lilah used pipe cleaners to mould letter shapes as she said them, she used water pistols to spell out words on the wall and put different letter-strings into balloons, then popped them before reading out the letter strings. Lilah wrote in sand, made letter shapes on her back and took time to get to know the shape of her face when she made the letter sounds. All of this was instead of only using a pen and paper, and talking through the sounds a few times in a relatively formal setting. Literacy had remained tricky for Lilah but those foundational years meant that she was able to learn to read and write independently, rather than always needing additional input.

Building the Early Foundations for Literacy

In this final section, I will look at some more general strategies to support children in the Early Years with different elements of their development. The strategies are grouped together in the same way as the challenges in the section above are, so that you can relate the challenges and ways to address them to each other.

Speaking and Sounds

When children have difficulties in their speech sounds you can help them by:

- Enunciating fully when you talk to them. Your accent doesn't matter but saying each letter and saying words clearly will help children to discern different sounds.
- Face them as you speak so they can link sounds to the shape of your mouth when you say them.
- Model sounds if children make mistakes when they speak. For example, repeating back 'they' in place of 'vey' so that children hear it.
- Play games like 'I Spy' using letter sounds but with the sounds being located at different points in words so that children must identify them.
- Playing rhyming games where children must identify words which are similar and different, with a discussion about why as part of the game.
- Some children may find TV shows such as *Alpha Blocks* helpful as they start to get to grips with their initial letter sounds. Watching this with them can help children get used to the sounds and you can talk them through while watching the programme.
- Singing nursery rhymes with children can be helpful or saying tongue-twisters as they encourage active, accurate listening, with clear speech needed for repetition of the target phrases.

Patterns and Orders

In any setting there are routines and patterns throughout the day, whether at home, work or school. These can be tricky for children to recall, particularly if they have difficulties in their working memory. Here are some strategies to help:

- Ordering the alphabet can be challenging for children. Using 3D letters and working with them can turn tasks into a multi-sensory experience.
- Games to recall orders can be useful. 'I Went to Market' is a classic alphabet and memory game, as are match-up games.
- Visual timetables and checklists can help children (and their parents!) know what they need to do, when and where. Visual equipment lists can also be used as needed in class.
- Google Home or Alexa devices can be helpful for children to remember things if they are programmed with appropriate information. They can even work for children in the Early Years!
- Pictures and talking through routines regularly can help children get to know them. Rehearsing tasks by walking through them before doing them 'officially' can also be useful.

Processing the World Around Us

Where children find processing information difficult, there are various strategies that might be helpful. Although dyslexia is generally linked to vulnerabilities in verbal processing, making sense of other information may also be tricky. Some strategies are below:

- Taking time while giving instructions so that children can process them one at a time. Once you've finished talking, give the group time and ask for one of them to repeat back the instructions you've given.
- Use multi-sensory prompts to help children make sense of spoken information. Use pictures of sounds/words so that they can associate the information with those different stimuli.
- Let children volunteer to answer questions rather than picking them and putting them on the spot. Time is key in helping them to make sense of tasks and process their own responses.
- Flow charts and prompt sheets can help children with routines and processes rather than expecting them to recall everything themselves. This can help them focus on new learning or other tasks rather than just recalling the routines.

Literacy Learning Journeys

> ### ❓ Reflection Point: My Practice and My Students
>
> You've had some time to work through this chapter and think about different ways that dyslexia may appear in young children. At the start of the chapter, we focussed on speech and language, which may have seemed a little unexpected. However, as we've worked through, links between speech and language and dyslexia/literacy difficulties have been built.
>
> Think about children you work with now (or perhaps your own children).
>
> - Do they have any wobbles in their speech and language?
> - Do you notice any of those wobbles influencing how they write or read?
> - Is there anything that you can do to help develop their speech and language, which may help their literacy development?
> - Can you think of any games or activities you can use to help them with processing or their memory?
>
> Go and try them!

Key Takeaways

- Speech and language difficulties are linked closely to dyslexia, and may be an early indicator of dyslexia or potential challenges with literacy. Schools are well-placed to identify these challenges and may be able to suggest strategies to use at home with children to boost their language skills.
- Memory and processing difficulties can be associated with dyslexia (and potentially other specific learning difficulties/neurodiversities). These can manifest in children having difficulties remembering songs and rhymes. Remembering sequences of information like days of the week, months of the year or instructions for tasks may also be tricky for them. Children may seem to be paying attention, and then not be able to recall what was said in class, or they may omit parts of instructions or information. They may also get distracted in tasks or forget what they are doing part way through.
- Processing speed is an area of difficulty for dyslexic people, so children who are at risk of dyslexia are likely to find making sense of verbal information tricky. Given that a lot of learning in the Early Years is done through play and talking, children who find it hard to make sense of information may not always be able to keep up with learning. They may miss instructions or not follow conversations completely. Slow processing speed can also mean that children need extra time to 'find' words themselves when they are speaking.
- Where children have weaknesses in phonological awareness, this complexity compounds the difficulties that they may have in starting to link letters to sounds (already challenging due to the complexity of English spelling). Early support in developing speech sounds and phonological awareness can help mitigate some of these difficulties.

Further Reading

- If you want to know about the different areas of development which are monitored by practitioners within the English setting, you can look at government frameworks here: https://www.gov.uk/early-years-foundation-stage.
- There is also non-statutory guidance that breaks down the whole Early Years phase into smaller, age-related chunks and presents the different targets within those age ranges according to the seven areas of development. This can be found here: https://assets.publishing.service.gov.uk/media/64e6002a20ae890014f26cbc/DfE_Development_Matters_Report_Sep2023.pdf.
- If you are concerned that your child or a child within your setting may have dyslexia, you can access a list of indicators and a checklist of the different manifestations of dyslexia in the Early Years here: https://www.bdadyslexia.org.uk/advice/children/is-my-child-dyslexic/signs-of-dyslexia-early-years.
- The publication *Early Help Better Future: A Guide to the Early Recognition of Dyslexia* by Jean Augur has some excellent information. It offers more detail and some informal exercises you can do with children in the Early Years to explore whether they may have any vulnerabilities in their profile that could indicate dyslexia. https://cdn.bdadyslexia.org.uk/uploads/documents/Advice/early-help-better-future.pdf?v=1554464143.
- The British Dyslexia Association and PATOSS have jointly published a guide for families to support their children. The publication called 'Understanding and supporting neurodiversity: Support strategies for parents and carers' offers practical strategies and further information about dyslexia in an accessible and easy-to-read format. It is available here: https://cdn.bdadyslexia.org.uk/uploads/documents/Advice/Webinar-Training/Support_strategies_for_all_parents_and_carers_250118_copy.pdf?v=1554825979.

References

Borleffs, E. *et al.* (2019) 'Cracking the code: The impact of orthographic transparency and morphological-syllabic complexity on reading and developmental Dyslexia'. *Frontiers in Psychology*, 9, p. 2534. https://doi.org/10.3389/fpsyg.2018.02534.

Cabbage, K.L. *et al.* (2018) 'Exploring the overlap between Dyslexia and speech sound production deficits'. *Language, Speech, and Hearing Services in Schools*, 49(4), pp. 774–786. https://doi.org/10.1044/2018_LSHSS-DYSLC-18-0008.

Daneman, M. and Merikle, P.M. (1996) 'Working memory and language comprehension: A meta-analysis', *Psychonomic Bulletin & Review*, 3(4), pp. 422–433. https://doi.org/10.3758/BF03214546.

Department for Education (DfE) (2023) 'Development matters - Non-statutory curriculum guidance for the early years foundation stage'. Available at: https://assets.publishing.service.gov.uk/media/64e6002a20ae890014f26cbc/DfE_Development_Matters_Report_Sep2023.pdf (Accessed: 26 April 2024).

Department for Education (DfE) and Department for Health (DfH) (2015) *Special Educational Needs and Disability Code of Practice: 0 to 25 Years*. London: DfE and DfH. Available at: https://assets.publishing.service.gov.uk/government/uploads/system/uploads/attachment_data/file/398815/SEND_Code_of_Practice_January_2015.pdf (Accessed: 5 August 2021).

Herrington, M.H. and Macken-Horarik, M. (2015) 'Linguistically informed teaching of spelling: Toward a relational approach'. *The Australian Journal of Language and Literacy*, 38(2), pp. 61–71. https://doi.org/10.1007/BF03651957.

Schwering, S.C. and MacDonald, M.C. (2020) 'Verbal working memory as emergent from language comprehension and production'. *Frontiers in Human Neuroscience*, 14, p. 68. https://doi.org/10.3389/fnhum.2020.00068.

UK Government (Undated) 'Early years foundation stage, GOV.UK'. Available at: https://www.gov.uk/early-years-foundation-stage (Accessed: 26 April 2024).

4
Dyslexia in Early Primary School

Introduction

In this chapter, we explore the effect on children of the change in approaches from the Early Years, into the more formalised learning journey that begins in Key Stage 1. Early Years learning and how it links to the Key Stage 1 curriculum is briefly touched upon and the differences between Key Stages are highlighted. The interaction of dyslexia and curricular expectations is explored, as well as the wider effects of dyslexia on young people with their engagement in activities outside school. You are given the opportunity to reflect on your own practice or even your own children at several points throughout this chapter. Those reflection points are throughout the chapter so you can draw on what you've read, and also refer to your previous thoughts on earlier questions as you work through the book.

The chapter briefly considers wellbeing and how it can be affected by dyslexia. Difficulties in wellbeing can already be seen in children as young as Key Stage 1, where they have challenges in accessing elements of the curriculum, or where they perceive themselves as different from their peers in many ways. The emotional effects of dyslexia have been documented widely (Nalavany et al., 2011; Tarrasch et al., 2016), and if not addressed and supported, they can impact young people as they move through school and on into adulthood (Nalavany et al., 2011). Understanding how young people respond to challenges in school (and out) can help us as practitioners to see where they may be struggling in other ways too.

> **? Reflection Point: *When Does Dyslexia 'Hit'?***
>
> In this box, we'll consider different skills and strengths that children have and how/when you start to notice them. Dyslexic-traits can be seen as early as six years old, and its effect on children can be huge!
>
> Take a moment. When do you start to see talents and areas of strength in young people? The child who can run faster than others? The gymnast? The little one, whose sense of rhythm and bopping sets them apart as a fantastic dancer? The other student whose singing turns heads?
>
> When do you start to nurture and build up those talents? Are they explained away as developmental and something that young people will grow out of or, just master and develop all by themselves without any input and support?
>
> So now, we'll think about challenges that young people experience. What do we do about the student who can't do their laces up, or the student who finds it hard to hold their pen? The student who doesn't always hear the difference between /th/ and /v/? The student whose sound-to-letter mapping just does not seem to stick?
>
> How are those children supported? Are their challenges brushed under the carpet and is it assumed that they'll be all right in due course? How does dyslexia fit into this?

Curriculum in Key Stage 1

Here, we look at how the curriculum shifts gear as students move into more formalised learning in Key Stage 1 from their Early Years setting. There are large differences in how the curriculum is broken down between Early Years and Key Stage 1, which link to the emphases on different elements of learning as children progress. We will link the Early Years Framework to Key Stage 1, focussing on different assessment points and strategies.

Literacy Learning Journeys

What Went Before

The Early Years Foundation Status (EYFS) Learning Goals are split into seven different areas, so that children can make a strong start in school, ready for their formal learning and be able to engage positively with their peers. At the end of Reception class, at the end of EYFS, teachers must compile an EYFS profile, which is an assessment of children's development, matched against 17 Learning Goals. The profiles are used by Year 1 teachers to understand where children are developmentally, so that they can support them effectively. It is also useful for parents and carers, so that they have an overview of their children's progress. The areas of development and Learning Goals are discussed briefly below, linked to the overarching curricular areas. Aside from literacy and maths, the curricular areas are not separated into academic subject areas.

> ## ❓ Reflection Point: Different Development Paths
>
> We are part way through the Early Years curriculum outline, which may seem an odd place to stop. However, it's deliberate.
>
> Speech and language can have a huge impact on literacy development, as we saw in Chapter 3, but we need to think about physical development too. Reflect on the following and consider if it may make literacy challenging:
>
> - Pen hold: How do children hold their pen?
> - Core strength and posture: How can this impact on writing?
> - Eyesight: Do children all see well in your class? May this impact on literacy?
> - Catching a ball: Can students catch a ball? Do they have trouble with their motor coordination? How could this impact literacy?
>
> Now think about any children in your setting who may have some or all of these challenges. What can you do so support them? What resources do you have? If you're not sure, who can you ask?
>
> Taking a moment to consider the holistic impact of dyslexic traits is important, particularly as students move from one phase to another. Spotting gaps in their skills early can make life infinitely easier in the long-term.

Communication and Language

There are two areas of focus within communication and language:

- Listening, attention and understanding
- Speaking

Each of these skills underpin children's access to other elements of the EYFS programme. Children need to be able to 'listen attentively and respond to what they hear' (DfE, 2023: 12), engaging in conversation with peers and teachers as they make sense of the learning. These discussions take place in groups, 1:1 and also as a whole class, where children develop their knowledge of vocabulary, explain their perspectives and reasoning for different things that happen, as well as sharing their creative ideas. Where young people find this tricky, other elements of learning can be challenging for them. Language skills underpin literacy skills; children need to be able to discern and articulate the different sounds in words, before they can start to relate them to letters.

Physical Development

This focusses on gross and fine motor skills. Where young people's gross motor skills do not develop as expected, they may have difficulties in navigating physical spaces. Weaknesses in strength and balance skills can impact on fine motor strength as posture is implicated in how children engage with the physical setting of their desks and learning. Holding a pencil in an effective, efficient grip is expected, as is the ability to use scissors and cutlery. Challenges here can have substantial and negative effects on young people's handwriting as they progress through to Key Stage 1.

Literacy

'Comprehension' of stories and narratives is expected; young people can show this through verbal explanation of ideas, anticipating what may happen in stories and also by using vocabulary they have heard in their own stories.

Reading and writing are expected too. Young people are expected to know a sound for each letter in the alphabet, as well as at least ten digraphs (two letters representing one sound). They should be able to read words which are consistent with their knowledge of phonics using blending skills. These skills map into their expected writing outcomes too. The expectation is that children should be able to write letters correctly so that they are recognisable, and where they write words, they should be able to link sounds to letters correctly, as part of phrases and sentences that others can recognise. These skills again underpin the work that young people will tackle as they move into Year 1, but to be able to link sounds to letters effectively, young people need to be able to speak them clearly and also listen. Their physical development, particularly fine motor skills, is linked to writing development too. When there are vulnerabilities here, the increasing challenges into Key Stage 1 can amplify vulnerabilities.

> **Maths in Practice**
>
> **Name:** Imogen
>
> **Age:** 7
>
> **What's tricky?** As well as finding literacy tricky, Imogen really struggles to remember her times tables and mental maths is really hard for her. She just can't hold all the different numbers and bits of sums in her head!
>
> **What's happening in school?** At the moment, Imogen is supported with her literacy. She has spellings and reading sessions three times a week but her maths hasn't been targeted yet, even though she is starting to fall behind and lose confidence. Imogen has always enjoyed the practical problem-solving bits of maths and loves reasoning tasks but remembering it all and then writing it down is very hard for her.
>
> **Why are things tricky?** Working memory can be at the root of maths challenges. Imogen's sense of numbers is excellent. She can count, understand different magnitudes and is able to use numbers to solve problems. Working memory is needed to hold more complex calculations and to do multi-step problems, and processing is implicated in multiplication table recall. These are both tricky for Imogen because she has dyslexia.

> **What can school do to help?** Give her time to make sense of tasks. Help her to note key facts, using highlighters, or noting numbers down on rough paper/mini-whiteboards. Let her talk through tasks. Let her use her fingers; they are attached to Imogen so let her use them if it helps her with recalling her maths facts!

What Follows On

In Key Stage 1, learning becomes more formalised with the national curriculum stipulating which subjects must be covered in England (other home nations have different programmes of study for children at the start of primary school), rather than overarching learning aims and areas of development. These are not discussed here explicitly but assessment strategies and shifts in curriculum emphases are highlighted.

Phonics and the Screener

The Key Stage 1 Phonics Screener is a statutory assessment usually taken in Year 1. Children read 40 words to their teacher, with teachers using the outcomes from this to feed into whether children may need extra support for their reading. If children don't meet expected standards in Year 1, they can redo the assessment in Year 2. In contrast to the formative progress tracking in EYFS, this is likely to be a child's first 'pass/fail' assessment. The emphasis on the screener can mean that children start to make comparisons between themselves and others, with their wellbeing sometimes being impacted.

Children may be aware that they find literacy tricky but the formality of the screener can be very stressful for them. Young children may be taken into smaller groups or set different work if they are finding literacy tricky. Whether this is before or after the Phonics Screener may vary, according to how different schools work and the format of additional support is also likely to differ, depending on the capacities of any given setting. But young people will understand that they find things tricky and will have already started to compare themselves to their peers.

Dyslexia in Early Primary School

Writing and Reading

Within the English curriculum at Key Stage 1, there are five areas (DfE, 2014):

- Word reading.
- Reading comprehension.
- Writing.
- Handwriting.
- Spoken language.

Word Reading

It is clear from the ordering of the skill areas, that there is a shift in the emphasis of the curriculum. Whereas spoken language was key in the EYFS Learning Goals, reading and writing takes centre stage in Key Stage 1. Young people are expected to demonstrate their phonics knowledge through decoding words, even where words do not follow regular spelling rules and may not be decodable using phonics alone. Young people are expected to read aloud and make sense of contractions in writing, as indicated through use of apostrophes. They are expected to know exception words (not decodable) and some basic suffixes. This differs substantially from their EYFS experiences and expectations, where they were very much working at letter level. Reading fluency is emphasised as a means for young people to develop their confidence in word reading, with the programme of study suggesting that this can be tackled through children rereading books they have already tackled.

> **? Reflection Point: Reading Comprehension and Loving Reading**
>
> Reading comprehension expectations state that young people should be taught to develop pleasure in reading (DfE, 2014) as the first element of reading comprehension. This is expected to develop motivation and engagement with reading. However, can we teach children to love something, or just how to do it?
>
> Speaking personally, I don't enjoy reading but I can do it. I see its value and purpose as a tool to access the wider world and knowledge. It can prompt imagination and creativity, but I don't love it and I never have. I find it incredibly hard. I wonder whether expecting that children will develop pleasure in reading may be putting unnecessary stress on them, particularly if they find it hard.
>
> Do we need to teach pleasure in reading or how to do it, with discussion of its benefits and how it may be fun or bring people together?
>
> There is no definitive answer here, but we need to be aware that it can be very difficult to enjoy something where there is an underlying barrier to being able to do it.

Writing and Spelling

Writing and spelling are emphasised in the Key Stage 1 curriculum with young people being expected to learn large numbers of words, add prefixes and suffixes, as well as adapt words to form different tenses. Letter naming is expected, as well as knowing different sounds that map onto various letters. Dictation is a skill expected within the curriculum framework. Where young people have difficulties discerning sounds or phonics, this will be inherently challenging for them.

Within handwriting expectations, posture is explicitly mentioned: Children should be able to sit correctly at a table (interestingly, 'correctly' is not defined within the programme of study). Lower and upper case letters should be formed and children are expected to be able to group different types of letters together. Motor skills are implicated here, as well as past experiences working at a table; not every child has access to a table they can sit at and do writing. There is acknowledgement of the potential challenges that left-handed children may have but again explicit guidance is not found within the main programme of study documentation.

Interestingly, and perhaps helpfully for students with dyslexia or literacy challenges, when composing their own writing, young people are expected to say their ideas aloud before starting to write. The sequence of words they'll use can be rehearsed verbally and they can discuss their ideas with others before writing. The slight downside of this process for dyslexic children is that they may have vulnerabilities in their verbal working memory, which can make sequencing their ideas very difficult. However, tools such as Talking Tins[1] can be useful for children to record their thoughts on and revisit as they need to.

There are substantial expectations for the application of vocabulary, spelling, punctuation and grammar, which can be very challenging for young people with dyslexia due to vulnerabilities in working memory, as well as the difficulties they may have with phonological awareness. While there is an importance to young people being able to write accurately and discernibly themselves, sometimes there may be emphasis on ideas rather than writing, or children may be able to use alternative recording strategies to show their understanding. Different support measures will be discussed below.

---

1 This is a type of voice recorder and can be useful for recording ideas in the classroom. They are available here: https://www.talkingproducts.com/collections/talking-tins-learning-resources (accessed 9 February 2024)

The Wider Curriculum

The wider curriculum in primary school relies increasingly on the written word as young people progress through. In England, the Key Stage 1 programme of study details compulsory subjects to be taught in school. These are noted as separate curriculum areas, and although they may be taught as part of a cross-curricular programme, the subjects are monitored separately in many schools. Subject-specific knowledge is taught, tested and monitored, with a large amount of this being conveyed by the written word. Although young people can, in principle, record their learning differently, this is not always the case in many schools.

Skills are taught alongside procedures which were used in EYFS and sequencing is a strong element of these skills. For example, in science, young people are expected to be able to observe and classify items, which both rely on working memory. The processes by which objects are classified requires knowledge and understanding of context. While the skills may be transferrable, knowledge becomes more specific in Key Stage 1. Dyslexic children may struggle to retain and/or retrieve learning which combined with challenges in literacy can make the curriculum increasingly tricky for them to access. This means that it is incredibly important for teachers to be aware of the impact of literacy challenges on young people and how to identify – and subsequently – support them. Families shared their journeys and different strategies they used to support their children when I was researching this book. Eleanor's story gives some insight into how one family worked on literacy outside of school, and the impact of this work inside of school.

> **Name:** Eleanor
>
> **Professional Role**: Head of English in a secondary school, and de facto dyslexia expert there
>
> **Dyslexic Connection**: Her son, Oscar, is severely dyslexic.
>
> **Location:** Southeast of England
>
> **His school type:** Maintained Infant School
>
> **What made school hard for him:** Oscar found it really hard to make progress in reading. He struggled to link letters to sounds, which meant that spelling was also really hard for him. During lockdowns, his family spent time on literacy, working through the Ruth Miskin Read Write Inc[2] phonics programme, which boosted Oscar's general literacy skills. Being able to read and write with more confidence helped Oscar feel more able to access the curriculum. Oscar found his literacy difficulties made other elements of learning very difficult for him, which really affected his self-esteem.
>
> **What did they do to help him:** The school supported each child that struggled in their literacy and did a huge amount of small group support. Oscar was also supported 1:1, which helped to boost his confidence. He was never singled out and made to feel different from other students, which meant that he could reinforce his phonics, develop his reading and spelling, and still be at ease with himself.
>
> **What was your experience of this school, as a family:** Eleanor and Oscar had an overall positive experience in his Infant School. Although he was a summer baby, which might have meant that

---

2 Details about the Read Write Inc Phonics Programme can be found here: https://www.ruthmiskin.com/programmes/phonics/ (accessed 27 January 2024)

> the school did not perceive him as having dyslexic-tendencies, the school did see that there were some underlying difficulties and acted accordingly. They talked his family through the challenges he had in learning and communicated effectively about how they were supporting Oscar. The school took time to forge a relationship with Oscar's family, which was beneficial for them all, as the team around Oscar!

Dyslexia Outside of Literacy

> **? Reflection Point: What Else Is Hit by Dyslexia?**
>
> One of the key aims of this book is to help you understand the different ways that dyslexia can show in children and young people at different stages along their path through education. So we are starting right at the beginning of formal learning. Have a think for a moment:
>
> - How might dyslexia affect other areas?
> - What might that look like in Key Stage 1 students?
> - How do you think the Delphi definition links to those areas?
>
> If it helps you, make a note of your thoughts somewhere so you can go back to them later and see if your initial thoughts still hold true.

This section will look at dyslexia and its wider impact in the first few years of primary school, known as Key Stage 1 in England and covering Years 1 and 2 (ages 5–7), or Years 2–3 in Northern Ireland. These years/ages are denoted differently within the other regions of the UK, with Scotland following the continuous Curriculum for Excellence from ages 3–18. Northern Ireland has its own curriculum but it is broken down into similar age bands as in England. In Wales, the Curriculum for Wales runs continuously from ages 3–16, as of 2022 (The School Run, no date). However, I think it is really important to keep in mind that different frameworks do not necessarily impact on the way in which young people develop. It may mean that different skills, knowledge and activities are expected at slightly different ages within those structures, but each curriculum has the aim of supporting children and young people to be their best selves, albeit potentially through different strategies and pedagogical philosophies. I will tend to cover the English systems more heavily than others because that it my experience but I will try, as I have in other chapters, to signpost you to useful resources for your areas.

Dyslexia has wide-reaching impacts on many areas of children's lives, which we have explored partially in the previous section about the Early Years. Here we will look at how dyslexia and how it starts to creep into other elements of young people's lives. We will see that right from the get-go, dyslexia is more than just a literacy 'thing'.

Ordering and Sequencing

Dyslexia impacts verbal memory, which can affect how people retain and order information given verbally or in written form. It is probably worth mentioning here however, that there are other neurodiversities where verbal and other elements of working memory are implicated, subsequently impacting ordering and sequencing. Dyslexia may not be the only reason young people find ordering and sequencing very tricky. So here, I think what is done to support dyslexics can be very helpful for other people.

I write here from personal experience and also professionally. Remembering anything in order is inexplicably difficult for me, and that was felt most prominently on the sports pitch: I could never remember the drills we were supposed to do. I always had to look at them and talk myself through things once or twice before I could join in properly. I don't remember how well I could order things, or sequence things particularly when I was in Key Stage 1, but I do have in mind that ballet really was not my thing! Darcey Bussell's experiences with dyslexia are discussed; dyslexia impacts all areas of life!

Sports, Dance and Other Activities

Remembering information is key in so many different things that young people do from an early age. I have taught children who have been exceptional athletes, many of whom were dyslexic and who felt that having another outlet for their talents was vital for their wellbeing as they progressed through school. Many activities rely on young people being able to make sense of long lists of instructions, and then they can be expected to just get on with whatever they have been told. This can resemble children's experiences in school, which can be incredibly detrimental to them when they are doing something they love!

Drills, rehearsals, technical language and sequences of movements are implicated in so many different activities that children may take up when they are very young. So making sure that those hobbies and activities build up children's confidence and skills rather than emphasising their difficulties is vital. Young people's experiences and talents outside of the classroom need be celebrated, whether they have dyslexia, wider SEND or not; the potential emotional impact of dyslexia cannot be understated (Antonelli et al., 2014). So those working with children outside of school do need to be aware of dyslexia and other learning needs, so that they can support those working with them through inclusive practice. As with many things, what works for dyslexic children often works well for other learners too.

Music and drama can also be important outlets for people who find some aspects of school-based learning tricky. The markers for 'success' differ and there is often flexibility in how children learn, whether they have chosen to do piano lessons or Saturday morning theatre class. This flexibility can be a lifeline for young people. There may be challenges with music such as having difficulty with sight reading, or needing more time to learn pieces (British Dyslexia Association (BDA), no date). However, the benefits and sense of success and confidence that children can gain is priceless. These skills can start to be developed in Key Stage 1 (I was seven years old when I started to have piano lessons!) and can reap rewards; children need to have an avenue where they can be successful and the arts or sports can be just that.

Name: Darcey Bussell

Year: Born in 1969

Location: London

School type: Darcey started school in her local primary school and was diagnosed with dyslexia when she was nine years old. She moved to the 'Arts Educational School', where she developed her stage and performance skills. Her 13–18 secondary education was completed at the Royal Ballet School, and she later joined the Royal Ballet Sadler's Wells company.

Main challenges in school: Darcey found reading and writing frustrating when she was little. She was behind in her learning and often felt like she couldn't express herself fully. Darcey has said in the media that her teachers often thought that she was lazy. She sometimes ran away to hide in cupboards rather than do writing tasks! Darcey spent a lot of time avoiding writing and if she did have to, she would often illustrate her task with a picture, focussing for so long on drawing that she would not have time to write more than a few lines in her story. She found tests hard and always felt that her spelling let her down when she was working in school. Her reading was a challenge and Darcey still finds it hard to read when she is preparing work with TV scripts.

Strengths: Despite finding learning very challenging, Darcey was a very determined learner. She worked hard on subjects like history and excelled at gymnastics. Darcey was even on the boys' football team when she was in primary school. Her mum sent her to ballet lessons and Darcey found her outlet. She applied her diligence and determination to dance.

Darcey and her dyslexia: Darcey was supported by her family to see the other talents she had, despite finding some things extremely challenging in school. She feels that if she hadn't had some of the challenges and negative experiences related to her dyslexia in school and along the way, that she would not be where she is today. She credits her grit and determination to the support she had at home, but Darcey (while recognising the challenges her dyslexia has brought her) does see the positive aspects of her dyslexia: It helped her find direction and what she really wanted to do!

What Are the Wobbles and What Can We Do about Them?

I am dyslexic and I have always done lots of sport. I spend a lot of time on my bike as a stressbuster, running helps with old injuries from various sports and rugby was a huge part of my life at university. The British Dyslexia Association (British Dyslexia Association (BDA), 2023) points to spatial awareness and visual thinking skills as strengths for many dyslexic people. This was also the case for Darcey Bussell and helped her to excel as a dancer. As I wrote above, it is really important to make sure that young people are supported to engage in activities where they can excel. Confidence boosting matters, so understanding where and how dyslexia can impact on young people in their 'fun' activities matters so they can be supported, and so the activities can stay fun! The difficulties young people may have here don't necessarily differ greatly from those they experience in the classroom but they need to be addressed, and can potentially be done far more flexibly.

Remembering or Understanding Instructions, Drills or Plays

Remembering verbal instructions is an area of challenge for dyslexics. When they are in Key Stage 1, it is important to support them by remembering information using other strategies. The reasons for this are various:

We want to start helping children develop strategies for remembering and making sense of instructions, they need to feel empowered as athletes, musicians or performers (depending on what they are doing), and they need to feel successful and valued. So if you're working with a child in Key Stage 1, now is the time to start talking to them about how they feel they best learn and remember things, and listen. They may want to:

- Watch others do something first.
- Talk through what you've asked them to do.
- Look at a video of something first.
- Note down key words from your instructions.

Here, in supporting children from a young age, not only are you teaching them their voices matter, but you are also supporting their metacognition. Metacognition in relation to their fun activities can be transferred into the classroom, so that young people start to understand themselves and how they can be successful. No age is too young for this, and I would wholly argue that working at Key Stage 1 to support children understanding and expressing their preferences is really important.

Not 'Getting' Things the First Time

Sports, the arts and other activities outside of the classroom can provide a setting for young people to develop transferable skills and a strong sense of self. The confidence-boosting opportunities within these settings give children a sense of success where they may not have the same experience in school. In Key Stage 1, children can already perceive the differences between themselves and their peers. They will see where they are not as strong, so supporting them to excel elsewhere can bolster their self-esteem when faced with challenges and support their wellbeing.

In my mind, there is a stereotype of a somewhat brutal sports coach who is intolerant of dissent and 'failure'. So sports can be a setting in which the stakes do seem very high for young people. They want to do well, and they want to be *seen* to do well. So here is where inclusive practice and time are their friends. There are many ways for young people to take new concepts or information on board, as I wrote above and it is so important for these to be 'normalised' outside the classroom or in it. Whatever sport or activity I've done over the years, I've invariably found it hard to make sense of things the first time I hear it. I could not sight-read musically if my life depended on it, and I cannot ever listen to instructions on how to perform a drill or play in sports training to then do it straight away. I've always needed to take time to process and make sense of things. So when a drill was explained, I could watch it and then do it. Music can also be an area where people need time to think things through before jumping straight into performing. It was certainly the case for me!

Helen and her Piano Exam

The context: In Year 13, at the same time as my A levels, I did grade 8 piano. I was good at piano and I enjoyed it. But I hated scales and sight-reading. I am terrible at both and I was lazy when it came to practising sight-reading. I have subsequently learned that it is something that dyslexics can find really tricky: processing, coordination and sequencing are all implicated.

The scene: I had played my pieces well, done the singing bit of the exam, which I was quite good at, and waded my way through the scales, very, very badly! Then I had to sight-read. It puts the fear of

> God into me; to this day I still tremble at the thought! I looked at the pages, practised the bits I could with separate hands and then my time was up. I fumbled a little, nearly cried and then told the examiner I couldn't do it.
>
> Now I realise that I could have had extra time in my exam to spend on sight-reading; processing and making sense of the tasks was hard. Getting both hands to do what I wanted at different times felt impossible so I gave up. I passed that exam by the skin of my teeth!

So Is it Dyslexia?

Dyslexia tends not to be formally identified in young people before they are seven years old. This does often mean that for most of Key Stage 1, young people do not have a formal diagnosis of dyslexia or other specific learning difficulties. However, it is possible to determine if there may be some tendencies towards dyslexia and/or other specific learning difficulties. As teachers, you can monitor your students' progress and determine whether they are meeting expected standards for their age group, where they are stronger and what their areas of vulnerability look like. Checks lists are available to identify potentially 'dyslexic' difficulties at different stages of education but they do not offer a definitive conclusion as to whether an individual has dyslexia or not. There are online screeners which give useful insight into a child's strengths and areas of challenge, which do give a snapshot into their profile. However, they are not an official 'diagnosis'.

The only way to determine whether a young person has dyslexia (or another specific learning difficulty) is via a formal, diagnostic assessment undertaken by a Specialist Assessor or appropriately qualified psychologist (usually Educational Psychologists do this work). That said, it is entirely possible to identify students for whom literacy development is difficult and to support them accordingly.

Supporting Literacy Development

The building blocks of literacy development in English are complex and where one area has vulnerabilities, often these can spill over into other parts of literacy and make progress in all elements of literacy challenging for children. Here we take a brief look at how to support children with some elements of literacy.

Phonics/Speech-to-Letter Sounds

While English is not a wholly phonics-based language, having a good understanding of the different sounds letters can make in English is a fundamental part of developing literacy skills. In the first instance, structured synthetic phonics programmes are helpful to start children along the pathway to reading, writing and spelling. There are online programmes, as well as paper-based programmes that can support this. The key thing to have in mind when selecting a strategy to support children who find phonics hard is that it needs to tie into whatever programme you use in class. Having multiple speech or sound patterns to consider in school can be too much for young people. It can be useful to consider the following as you choose phonics programmes and support strategies for your students:

- Who will deliver them and where?
- Which children will be implicated?
- Is the programme approved by the government and/or evidence-based? (There may be funding attached if the programme is.)
- Can it be delivered little and often?
- How will you monitor progress/impact?
- Can parents support children at home?

Constant exposure to the same thing, repeatedly, can be detrimental to young people's engagement with literacy and their wellbeing over time, particularly if their progress stagnates. When looking at phonics programmes, do look at what is different from what you have been doing previously to support your children.

Reading and Spelling

In Key Stage 1, often phonics programmes are the same as reading and spelling programmes. Many online packages deliver phonics input, as well as giving structured phonics input for young people. Reading and spelling can be taught concurrently using phonics and through learning English-language spelling conventions. In addition to phonological approaches to reading and spelling, morphological approaches can be useful. This is particularly important to consider as Key Stage 1 curriculum requirements do make reference to prefixes and suffixes, as well as different tenses in verbs being addressed; knowledge of the 'shape' of language (morphology) can help here. While phonics-shaped chunks – otherwise known as phonemes – are very useful in English, because of its complex etymology and development other chunks can be helpful in supporting people to access the written word.

Writing

There are several elements that contribute to the process of writing, and they can be addressed differently so that children can be supported effectively, even in Key Stage 1! The physical act of letter formation can be very tricky for children, particularly for those younger in the year; the bone joints in their hands are younger and less developed. You can support children in letter formation with a few basic ideas:

- Pen grips.
- Fine motor skills boosting activities such as bead threading, pompom making, colouring etc.
- Using mini-whiteboards to practice letter forms.
- 3D letters so that children start to 'feel' them.
- Allow them time to process tasks.
- Writing practice classes/groups.

Planning skills and alternative recording strategies can also impact on writing. Using different tools and presenting strategies to children right from when they start literacy can be very helpful. Talking ideas through can be useful but sometimes children may need to have pictorial prompts, like when using mini-whiteboards. Worked examples or sentence-starters are fairly common planning methods and can be adapted according to children's age and the task at hand.

Boosting the 'Whole' Child and Their Wellbeing

Much work exists that discusses children's wellbeing and I touch on this throughout the book. Early identification of need is vital so that young people can be supported and find ways around their challenges, so they can make progress. How support is delivered can have a lasting impact on children's wellbeing and engagement with learning. Within the SEND Code of Practice (DfE and DfH, 2015), meaningful consideration of children's views is a key tenant of how support strategies can be developed and implemented. Some children may be happy to talk about their challenges in front of others. Other children may not want to publicly acknowledge the challenges they have, so their needs and wishes must be held differently. When working with young children, boosting their confidence and nurturing their strengths is vital; they are starting to be aware of their challenges. You might consider the following methods:

- Using buff paper for all students.
- Volunteering to read rather than being called upon.
- Student-selected learning partners to help with planning.
- In-class support where possible.
- Additional input for all children in groups, according to their vulnerabilities, or where they need challenging.
- Alternative recording and planning strategies; does everything need to be written down?
- Reset time for if students need a moment to calm down but make this available to all students, as and when they need it.

Key Takeaways

- Dyslexia can have wide-ranging impacts, even for young children. Children, whatever their age, know the things that they are good at and then know where they struggle. Challenges in literacy can seem insurmountable for children in Key Stage 1, where they may feel bombarded by the written word and tasks they just cannot access!
- Early identification of challenges and supportive intervention to support children with their areas of challenge is vital but alongside that, children need to feel successful. The areas where they do excel need to be highlighted and children need to feel that the skills they *do* have are seen.
- There are many ways to support literacy challenges, whether that is with teaching assistant-led support strategies, precision teaching, word maps or even online intervention packages.
- How you and your school choose to support your students will vary according to what you have in place for literacy instruction in the mainstream classroom, your staff skills and the needs of your students. What looks good and works in one setting may fall flat in another setting.
- Key to supporting children is looking at progress, how it is monitored and finding other ways in which children are not making progress. Alongside this, wellbeing and supporting children to thrive and be happy is vital; no one can learn if they are fundamentally unhappy in their setting. Getting this right and building confidence early can reap rewards later on.

Further Reading

- There are some substantive differences in how the school curricula are structured across the four regionss of the UK, and what is expected at different points along these journeys. This website gives a good and simple overview of the curricula with further reading suggestions if you want to look something up in more detail. https://www.theschoolrun.com/primary-education-england-wales-scotland-and-n-ireland (accessed 27 January 2024).
- The English Early Years Foundation Stage statutory framework can be found here: https://www.gov.uk/government/publications/early-years-foundation-stage-framework--2 and may be useful for you if you are working with young people in Key Stage 1 or if you are looking to understand how your child is progressing relative to expected levels/competencies (accessed 9 February 2024).
- The importance of sport can be looked at through the eyes of an athlete here. The article is about the personal challenges experienced by an Arizona-based NFL player, and gives real insight into the challenges he experienced in school. The article can be found here: https://cronkitenews.azpbs.org/2023/05/08/dyslexia-sports-new-way-academy-phoenix/ (accessed 27 January 2024).
- There is a similar story here, from a UK-based perspective. There is an article, and also a really inspiring video. It shows the powerful impact that sport can have on young people whose confidence is wobbling. You can find the video here: https://www.vivacombatathletics.co.uk/combat-sports-dyslexia/ (accessed 27 January 2024).
- Darcey Bussell is a dancer and her story is here. There are some videos and also an article that explores her journey. Sharing this could help give you ideas to inspire your learners as they start to discover their talents. You can find the article here: https://uk.style.yahoo.com/darcey-bussell-ballet-revelation-dyslexia-struggle-131155260.html (accessed 27 January 2024).

References and Bibliography

Antonelli, L. *et al.* (2014) 'Drama, performance ethnography, and self-esteem: Listening to youngsters with Dyslexia and their parents'. *SAGE Open*, 4(2), p. 215824401453469. https://doi.org/10.1177/2158244014534696.

British Dyslexia Association (BDA) (2023) *Sport and Dyslexia*. British Dyslexia Association. Available at: https://www.bdadyslexia.org.uk/news/sport-and-dyslexia (Accessed: 27 January 2024).

British Dyslexia Association (BDA) (no date) *Music and Dyslexia*. British Dyslexia Association. Available at: https://www.bdadyslexia.org.uk/advice/adults/music-and-dyslexia-1 (Accessed: 27 January 2024).

Department for Education (DfE) (2014) 'National curriculum in England: English programmes of study, GOV.UK'. Available at: https://www.gov.uk/government/publications/national-curriculum-in-england-english-programmes-of-study/national-curriculum-in-england-english-programmes-of-study (Accessed: 7 July 2023).

Department for Education (DfE) (2023) 'Early years foundation stage statutory framework for group and school-based providers'. *HMSO*. Available at: https://assets.publishing.service.gov.uk/media/65aa5e42ed27ca001327b2c7/EYFS_statutory_framework_for_group_and_school_based_providers.pdf (Accessed: 9 February 2024).

Department for Education (DfE) and Department for Health (DfH) (2015) *Special Educational Needs and Disability Code of Practice: 0 to 25 Years*. London: DfE and DfH. Available at: https://assets.publishing.service.gov.uk/government/uploads/system/uploads/attachment_data/file/398815/SEND_Code_of_Practice_January_2015.pdf (Accessed: 5 August 2021).

Nalavany, B.A., Carawan, L.W. and Brown, L.J. (2011) 'Considering the role of traditional and specialist schools: do school experiences impact the emotional well-being and self-esteem of adults with dyslexia?' *British Journal of Special Education*, 38(4), pp. 191–200. https://doi.org/10.1111/j.1467-8578.2011.00523.x.

Tarrasch, R., Berman, Z. and Friedmann, N. (2016) 'Mindful reading: Mindfulness meditation helps keep readers with Dyslexia and ADHD on the lexical track'. *Frontiers in Psychology*, 7. Available at: https://www.frontiersin.org/articles/10.3389/fpsyg.2016.00578 (Accessed: 20 April 2023).

The School Run (no date) 'Primary education in England, Wales, Scotland and N Ireland'. *TheSchoolRun*. Available at: https://www.theschoolrun.com/primary-education-england-wales-scotland-and-n-ireland (Accessed: 27 January 2024).

5
Dyslexia in Later Primary School

Introduction

The impact felt by young people with dyslexia can become more pronounced as they progress through school, with social settings as well as academic demands sometimes exacerbating or highlighting the differences in how they process and make sense of the world around them.

Key Stage 2 (ages 7–11) sees many changes across the curriculum. Young people will tackle increasingly complex subjects with a greater reliance on their literacy skills. They will often have to formally record their responses to tasks in writing, with much learning reliant on children's ability to read/write independently. While in primary school a lot of young people across Key Stage 2 are supported through targeted support in small groups, which can be a total game-changer. However, this does not necessarily help everyone to make the progress and gain the literacy skills needed to engage meaningfully in the curriculum. The reasons for this are myriad and are linked to wider structural constraints that schools are subject to, rather than through lack of desire to support learners.

The social milestones that young people go through in Key Stage 2 are also often substantially impacted by different learning challenges and needs. For instance, young people may start to travel to school with friends as they progress through school, or they may have residential trips with their classmates. These activities can place a substantial burden on them, as they have to navigate the changes in routine without the potential support of their parents/carers. On the playground, friendship groups can gain importance outside of young people's home setting and keeping up with friends can be challenging when young people find processing verbal information difficult. However, there are ways that young people can be supported to navigate these social and academic challenges as they start Key Stage 2 in Year 3 and

Dyslexia in Later Primary School

move towards Key Stage 3 at the end of Year 6. In looking at ways to support children through Key Stage 2, this chapter will cover the following:

- The differences in curriculum between Key Stages 1 and 2, and associated challenges.
- A case study to showcase the impact of teachers and their awareness, as children progress through school and beyond.
- How dyslexia can impact across the curriculum, looking at strengths as well as areas of challenge.
- Discussion of the effects of dyslexia on wellbeing and mental health.
- Support strategies and practical tips to help young people develop the skills they need as they progress towards secondary school.

❓ Reflection Point: Where Are Your Students at Just Now?

We are starting to look at a point in education where young people experience a lot of challenges. Their world is family-centric during their Early Years and Key Stage 1, but their focus moves towards their peers in Key Stage 2 as they gain independence and work towards secondary school. Young people change a lot over the four years which make up Key Stage 2, so understanding where young people are holistically at the start of Year 3 (or wherever they are when you are working with them) is really helpful. While you may not be working with young people in Key Stage 2 at the moment, it is sometimes helpful to consider points of change or transition when you work with them. With this reflection box, you may find it helpful to swap out 'Key Stage 1' and add in the age group you are working with; children develop a lot and there are always changes in the pipeline!

Consider any students in your class who have dyslexia or whose profile may be consistent with specific learning difficulties and reflect on the following questions/comments. You may find it helpful to make notes on your thoughts here, so that you can refer back to them as you read through the book, or even as you start to develop ways to support them.

- What were they really good at in Key Stage 1 and what did they enjoy? (These two things may not coincide!)
- How did their last teacher support them and what impact did it have?
- What do they find tricky and why? (For this one it can be a good idea to talk to the children and their parents/carers too).
- What external support (if applicable) is in place, or has been in place to support your students?
- What hobbies or interests do they have? Getting to know your students holistically is really helpful when building relationships with them, their families and other educators so that you can start to share common ground.

Curriculum Changes in Key Stage 2: Upping the Game

As young people progress through school and progress across Key Stages, they experience substantial changes in how they are expected to work, the emphasis of the curriculum and also with their social development. In this section, the focus is on the written word, rather than on the speaking and listening elements of the English Programme of Study. That is not to say that those skills are not important but the effects on students with speaking and listening difficulties linked to dyslexia will be addressed later in the chapter.

In Key Stage 1, there is a strong focus on young people developing their literacy skills so that they can read and work out the meanings of words they haven't yet encountered. Students are initially taught to write individual words, which then builds the skillset for them to be able to write in short sentences. As they progress into Key Stage 2, the demands on young people's literacy skills increase. They are expected to be able to read more in-depth texts, address comprehension questions about those texts and also use those texts to help them gain a broader understanding of concepts. When writing in Key Stage 2, young people are expected not only to use their complex, accurately punctuated, well-structured sentences in literacy sessions, they are also expected to use their literacy skills to write and express their ideas across the curriculum in other subjects. This section will give more detail about the demands of the Key Stage 2 curriculum compared with Key Stage 1, focussing on literacy skills but also broader skills, where working memory and information processing are implicated. Key Stage 2 is split into lower (Years 3 and 4) and upper (Years 5 and 6); these different stages will also be addressed because young people develop a lot over this time.

Reading Skills

Across Key Stages 1 and 2, reading is divided into word reading, which focusses on the mechanics and technicality of decoding words to be able to read them, and reading comprehension. There are set lists of words that young people are expected to be able to read at each stage and year group, which are set by the curriculum. Reading comprehension is a separate area for assessment and is broken down into two elements. Young people are explicitly expected to develop positive attitudes to reading, having developed, 'pleasure in reading, motivation to read, vocabulary and understanding' (Department for Education (DfE), 2013a) at the end of Key Stage 1. The potential impact of these expectations for young people with literacy difficulties is explored later in this chapter. Here, the different expectations are outlined and contextualised for young people in Lower and Upper Key Stage 2.

Lower Key Stage 2

Word Reading

At the end of Key Stage 1, young people will have largely worked using their phonics skills, which is to say that many of the words they have been learning can be decoded using regular phonics rules, where exceptions are not applicable. They will have encountered exception words, which cannot be decoded using phonics but which are frequently in passages that they work with in school. The exception words are noted in the Programme of Study for English (DfE, 2013a) and examples are given of different words for each year group/Key Stage.

In Year 3 the focus of word reading moves away from monitoring the blending skills and decoding of words at sound/letter level, towards a morphological approach. This involves young people exploring roots of words, prefixes and suffixes, and their effect on different words. There are lists of the expected roots, prefixes and suffixes of words within the relevant programmes of study for Years 3 and 4. Young people's knowledge of exception words continues to be monitored, with students being expected to know links between sometimes unexpected sounds and spellings in those words.

Reading Comprehension

At the end of Key Stage 1, young people are expected to have encountered a variety of types of texts such as poetry, stories and non-fiction passages which support them in being motivated to read, developing their vocabulary and general understanding of the world. It is also expected that young people find enjoyment in reading through this exposure to texts. In Key

Stage 2, young people are still expected to encounter a large range of types of text, which they may listen to or watch, as well as read. Engagement with texts moves from discussion of books to identification of themes, exploring the different phrases and words that have been used in passages to engage readers and using dictionaries to help them make sense of unfamiliar words.

Young people's understanding of passages is monitored through discussions, question exchanges and use of inference/prediction around what they have read, as they progress towards the end of Key Stage 1. This is still expected in Lower Key Stage 2 but the level of inference and prediction for example, is more detailed. Students are expected to be able to infer characters' thoughts, feelings and motives, and be able to draw on evidence for their views in the text. Summarisation is expected and young people are expected to be able to discuss language, structural and presentation choices made by writers, alongside the effects of those choices. It is expected that young people can retrieve and 'record' information from non-fiction texts. It is important to note here, that *how* information and understanding are demonstrated is not proscribed or detailed.

Upper Key Stage 2

Word Reading

In Upper Key Stage 2, it is largely expected that young people are equipped to decode unfamiliar words, whether using their knowledge of phonics or a more holistic, morphological approach. Within the Upper Key Stage 2 programme of study and expected standards, there is not explicit reference to learning new exception words. However, there are further words listed that young people are expected to learn as they progress through Years 5 and 6. The single expectation at this stage which relates to word reading is that young people apply their growing knowledge of morphological approaches to new words to help them make sense of those words.

Reading Comprehension

A significant expectation within the English programme of study for Upper Key Stage 2 is that young people are expected to learn a wide range of poetry by heart as part of their reading comprehension tasks. The programme of study also makes reference to the importance of poetry and reading comprehension in fostering children's positive attitudes to reading. They are expected to start making comparisons across books and other types of literature. While performance of poems and play scripts is in the English programme of study for reading comprehension in Key Stage 1 and Lower Key Stage 2, young people are expected to show their understanding of passages through tone, intonation and volume in Key Stage 2. Children are also expected to actively consider how an audience would make sense of their performance in Upper Key Stage 2. Children are expected to cater to a particular audience, which is part of supporting students' positive experiences with literature and reading.

To be able to make sense of passages and offer insights about them, young people in Upper Key Stage 2 are assumed to be able to decode and access the passages without difficulty. Young people are expected to discern between facts and opinions and make sense of non-fiction passages. The ways in which young people can show their understanding are also described, with some strategies such as writing, debates and using notes, whereas this is not the case for younger children. Young people are also expected to demonstrate their thought processes and explain the reason for their views across paragraphs, texts and across books/ publications.

Writing

Lower Key Stage 2

Spelling, Punctuation and Grammar

Children enter Lower Key Stage 2 with the expectation that they can spell common exception words, are able to spell regular, short words and link letters to their sounds effectively. Contracted forms of words are likely to have been introduced, as well as some suffixes and prefixes; these are detailed within the Programme of Study for English (Department for Education (DfE), 2013a). Dictation also features, with writing from memory also being an area of focus. Different types of sentences and clauses are areas where young people should have understanding of how to denote them, such as subordinate clauses or expanded noun phrases. Young people are introduced to homophones and possessive apostrophes, as well as writing sentences which are dictated by their teachers. Tenses are introduced in writing and various other, more complex, grammatical constructions as well as the technical language linked to those constructions which are also covered in Lower Key Stage 2.

Handwriting and Composition

At the end of Key Stage 1, children are expected to be able to form lower case letters of the right size, relatively, and to use appropriate lead-ins for joining letters together where appropriate, with consistent spacing between words and letters relative to the size of the writing. Focus is on accurate and consistent mark-making. As they progress through Lower Key Stage 2, young people are expected to be able to discern which letters should be joined and which are not, when they are adjacent to each other. The accuracy of strokes and general mark-making is expected to be refined, with lines being parallel where possible, so that ascenders/descenders do not touch across lines.

   The expectations around writing composition in Key Stage 1, much as with reading are about building foundations for young people to experience writing positively. They can write about personal experiences and use narratives, whether real or imaginary. Different forms of writing are developed and a formation of basic planning strategies begins. Talking through plans is noted as a way for young people to plan their ideas, as well as noting key words. As they progress through to Lower Key Stage 2, expectations linked to writing do not focus on enjoyment and developing positive experiences. Rather the focus shifts to young people starting to plan their writing, using discussion as well as recording their ideas. They are expected to draft their ideas and then evaluate and edit them, both through looking at their own work and other people's too. They are also expected to read work aloud in front of others, whether the class or a small group, with control over the tone and volume to make the meaning of passages clear. Young people are also expected to make alternative choices in their structures and vocabulary as part of the editing process. For children who have difficulties in their literacy, this can be very challenging; sharing written their work lays their vulnerabilities bare for others to see and commenting on others' work assumes that they can access other people's handwriting.

Upper Key Stage 2

Spelling, Punctuation and Grammar

An element of spelling and grammar that is not formally addressed prior to Upper Key Stage 2 is silent letters on words. This is challenging for young people developing the skills to use a dictionary to find spellings of unknown words. As with many elements of spelling, punctuation and grammar, these skills rely on young people being able to read what is written in the dictionary, remember spellings and make sense of new spellings, all under time pressure in a classroom setting.

Handwriting and Composition

Writing expectations in Years 5 and 6 are much less prescriptive and it is expected that young people have the mechanics of letter formation in place and can form their letters well. By this stage of primary school, young people are expected to be able to choose what tool they use to carry out their writing tasks, depending on the nature of the particular activities they are working on. Writing is moving towards young people having choices in how they form their letters, depending on the particular letter formations they have been shown. Young people are also freer to decide whether they join their letters or not.

When planning writing in Upper Key Stage 2, as with reading, the audience for the piece is expected to be considered during the planning and drafting phase. Young people are expected to write in an appropriate tone for the audience and vary their language according to the task. Their writing is expected to include literary devices which are chosen for a specific effect and evaluation should include proof-reading and ensuring that elements such as tense are consistent throughout the piece. Grammar and punctuation rules that young people use in Years 5 and 6 become increasingly technical, and they are expected to know the language linked to the structures, as well as to apply them accurately.

Reflection Point: Do Young People Need to Love Reading or 'Just' Be Able to Do It?

Within the primary school programme for English, there is a strong emphasis on young people being taught to love reading and to read for pleasure. There is a substantial body of research highlighting the benefits of reading for young people, and where they enjoy that reading, it reaps rewards for them both academically and socially. However, there are young people for whom reading does not come easily. This reflection point is here and is also a personal nod to the young people who don't like to read but understand its importance. So here, think on the following:

- Are there children in your class who do read because it is asked of them but do not do more than what is asked?
- Have those children ever said that they don't like to read? Might there be something that is making it hard for them?
- Do young people need to love reading? How do they view reading as a task – is it a means to an end or something they do as a fun activity?

> For those points, there is no right or wrong answer (despite what the curriculum says!). There are the answers that your students give, in the moment they give it, and that response may change over time. For some young people, the expectation that they will love reading and that they must read for pleasure can be a substantial cause of stress and pressure, which detracts from reading and may even demotivate them.
>
> For some, reading may be a tool and not something they choose to do outside of that. It is really important to leave young people that freedom too.

Literacy Across the Curriculum in Key Stage 2

Particularly towards the upper years in Key Stage 2, young people are expected to be able to express their views through the written word and to use passages of text to help enhance their understanding of topics. Government guidance (DfE, 2013b) notes that all aspects of literacy, including spoken language, should be developed as part of every school subject in Key Stage 2. The importance of spoken fluency in the language is also noted with explicit emphasis placed on young people being able to speak clearly and convey their ideas with confidence, using an appropriate register of language. Reading and writing development in all subjects is expected to develop language and acquisition of knowledge so that young people can access the curriculum and deepen their understanding of it.

The emphasis on using the written word and how work is pitched increases as young people progress through Key Stage 2, which can mean that young people who experience challenges around their literacy development are disadvantaged relative to their peers. The challenges linked to dyslexia and other literacy difficulties across Key Stage 2 are discussed below, alongside ways to reduce their impact on attainment and to support students' progress. Case studies are used here to share some people's lived experiences of Key Stage 2. Positive and negative journeys are shared, as well as insight into how teachers can support young people with dyslexia and literacy difficulties.

Dyslexia in Key Stage 2

As we have seen elsewhere in this book, dyslexia does affect reading, writing and spelling but there are also effects on other elements of young people's educational journey. Academic progress can be impacted as they struggle to access questions and/or commit their ideas to writing. In addition to academic barriers, young people may also experience challenges in social elements of school, and their wellbeing may also be impacted. These varied experiences will be addressed here.

Name: Sadie

Current occupation: Specialist Dyslexia Teacher

Learning history: Sadie found remembering things very difficult in primary school. Her working memory was weak, so copying from the board was tricky. Her teachers did not see her as academically bright because she did not always follow what was written on the board, or understand/remember instructions. She sat at the back of the classroom and wasn't challenged academically.

Since leaving school Sadie has been identified as having dyspraxia (DCD) and dyslexia, with particular vulnerabilities in her working memory and verbal processing.

Positive school experiences: Sadie enjoyed reading and was well-behaved at school, so teachers were generally kind to her.

Negative school experiences: Sadie was made to feel a failure when she was in school. She did not read easily until she engaged with Enid Blyton books, which she did enjoy. However, her teacher when she was nine or ten years old did not support her in learning. Sadie said that she was largely ignored at this stage when sitting at the back. Even when she was looking at the board, Sadie said that she was probably 'away with the fairies' and did not always know what was going on in the classroom.

Thoughts now: Sadie trained to be a primary school teacher and started to work in the Learning Support Department of a small independent school in the south of England. Part of her motivation for training to be a specialist dyslexia teacher was to support young people whose journeys through education were not always straightforward. Her negative experiences in primary school, particularly from the ages of 9–11 have inspired her to work to improve young people's journeys and to advocate for them. Sadie commented that a large proportion of her work is given to liaising between teachers and students to ensure that young people get the appropriate support so they can access the curriculum properly. She also highlighted the importance of the work she does 1:1 with students who have literacy difficulties. Often, Sadie finds that young people need to have time and space to air their difficulties in a non-judgemental setting. Sometimes very little curricular work takes place in her sessions, but young people benefit from the positive relationships they share and the advocacy that Sadie undertakes. She hopes that the need for her to advocate and argue on behalf of young people will reduce over time, as teachers' and other educators' general understanding and training relating to dyslexia/literacy challenges improves.

Some thoughts/questions for you:
Sadly, Sadie's experience in education is not uncommon. Her stories echoed in my research for this book and in my professional practice on an almost daily basis.

- Are there any children you work with who find remembering things tricky? Do they sometimes seem to lose track of instructions? Is there anything you can do to support them?
- Think about the quieter children in your group. Are they all fully engaged in learning? Do you talk to them and check in with how they're getting on? Do they have any struggles?
- What can you do to support those quieter children, who are bright and work hard but may not be reaching their potential?
- How can you incorporate confidence-building, self-esteem boosting moments into your teaching so that every child can have moments of success in their learning? These do not need to be huge celebrations but may just be being able to tick things successfully completed off a checklist.

Dyslexia and Reading

> Reading is one of the skills that many people associate with dyslexia. People are often aware that the underlying vulnerabilities in people's phonological or verbal skills can impact very visibly and tangibly on reading (see Chapter 2 for more information on what dyslexia is). As young people progress through Key Stage 2, they are expected to develop their reading skills and develop automaticity in decoding. That automaticity of decoding is expected to support improvements in reading fluency which then underpins young people's access to passages of text.

Where young people have not mastered the elements of reading tackled in Key Stage 1, they are likely to have substantial challenges in developing the fluency and decoding capacity expected as they work through Key Stage 2. Challenges in those areas can then mean that young people's reading comprehension skills are not as strong as others their age. Where young people have weaknesses in the skills underpinning reading, they may find that they lose their place in texts, or hesitate when they read aloud. This is where awareness of young people's difficulties is vital; although the programme of study does expect that young people are able to read publicly, doing so may be actively detrimental to those who have dyslexia.

At the level of comprehension, as passages become more challenging for students, they may be able to decode at word level, but in doing so, students may have to exert a lot of effort and subsequently lose the thread of what they have read. They may find they have missed important elements of passages, which can impact on their overall understanding of topics. The implications of these challenges are substantial given that reading and literacy are expected to be developed in all subjects across the curriculum in Key Stage 2, with reading playing a key part in students developing wider understandings of topics. Young people's progress may be limited as they find making sense of the written word increasingly challenging as the technical difficulty of passages increases.

Dyslexia and Writing

Writing is cognitively a very demanding process. Whether young people are copying notes from the board, writing information from memory or composing their own prose, if there are vulnerabilities in elements of the underpinning skills linked to writing, it may be very challenging for young people to demonstrate their knowledge effectively and fully use the written word. Like reading, the Programme of Study for English (DfE, 2013a) expects that many of the skills associated with writing and spelling have been mastered towards the end of Key Stage 1. Young people's phonics skills are expected to be of a level where they can spell regular words with ease and know how to write exception words, without hesitation. A level of automaticity and fluency of process is expected that may not have yet been reached by dyslexic students. This can have substantial impacts on young people's ability to fulfil the age-related criteria both at Lower and Upper Key Stage 2.

If a student focusses on their spellings, it may be that they are not able to form their letters as smoothly and consistently join certain groupings. If spelling is an area of struggle and young people are trying concurrently to work on their punctuation and grammar, they may not always manage to address both areas with full success. Sometimes, in focussing on spelling, grammar and development of new structures in writing, such as subordinate clauses or fronted adverbials, young people are not able to produce as much writing as others. This can mean that they are not able to show their understanding as well as others, despite perhaps being able to explain their understanding verbally or through the use of images. However, as is noted in the curriculum, young people may demonstrate their understanding of passages through discussion or questioning; although it is expected that they 'record' their learning, a specific method for doing so is not specified, which does provide flexibility and other options for young people and those working with them.

Dyslexia and Memory

Young people with dyslexia often experience challenges with elements of their verbal memory. Whether it is their short-term memory or their working memory, there is likely to be a tangible impact on how young people are able to engage with the curriculum. Short-term memory is often an area that young people find tricky (Tijms, 2004). This is the space where information is kept in sequence but not manipulated. Weaknesses here can impact directly on spellings; young people may not recall spellings even if they are given verbally to them, as they may not be able to retain all the letters.

Before content is addressed in writing tasks, weaknesses in spelling limit children's attainment and their ability to meet the Key Stage 2 expected outcomes. Instructions or lists of items are also likely to be tricky for young people to remember, which then starts to impact on other elements of the curriculum. Sequencing and retaining information impacts on young people's ability to recall elements of stories and their ability to summarise. This is also linked to weaknesses in working memory, which is the space where information is kept and concurrently manipulated. Both reading and writing can be impacted by vulnerabilities in working memory; decoding written passages and retaining their content can be very challenging, which can impact across the curriculum. In the same way, holding ideas for writing whilst juggling spellings and word order can mean that young people's writing does not flow as well or they may find it tricky to write as much as their peers. Weaknesses in memory can thus make learning new ideas and concepts difficult, as well as making it hard to share understanding and learning in the written form. There are also implications for retrieval of learning from long-term memory, which links to processing information.

Dyslexia and Processing

Processing information is implicated in all aspects of life. Whether in the classroom where young people are learning new concepts and retrieving prior learning, or in the playground with their peers, young people have to process information of some type. Challenges in verbal processing are an area directly linked to dyslexia. Verbal processing links to reading and writing, as well as speaking and listening, and accessing verbal concepts/ words is implicated in all of these areas. Verbal processing can be likened to filing information in and out of long-term memory, whether written, spoken or read.

In the classroom in Key Stage 2, there is a substantial emphasis on oracy skills, as a foundational element to literacy development. In primary school, young people may have had speech and language difficulties which can be linked to challenges in word finding. Where young people struggle to 'find' the word they want to use, they may have vulnerabilities in their verbal processing. This impacts on speech and writing, as well as reading. Verbal processing difficulties can also be linked to difficulties in making sense of instructions and concepts. As the technicality of tasks and subjects increases through Key Stage 2, young people may have fewer cues to rely on. For example, where their teacher may have given pictorial prompts in Key Stage 1, prompts may be verbal or written, which may be tricky for students to follow or process. If instructions are verbal, young people may find making sense of them difficult and whilst they are taking time to do so, they may miss input from their teacher.

Supporting Academics in the Key Stage 2 Classroom

The landscape for implementing support strategies into the classroom differs substantially in primary school compared with a secondary school. There are also differences between Key Stages 1 and 2 in how support may be implemented. The differences in strategies often reflect both developmental differences for young people and also the changing expectations of the curriculum. As with all strategies to support young people in any education setting, it is vital that the setting is clear on what the standard offer for young people with literacy challenges is, and what is 'reasonably' feasible with the setting at a given time. This is to ensure that the setting is compliant with both the Equality Act 2010 (HMSO, 2010) and the SEND Code of Practice

(DfE and DfH, 2015), which are the legal frameworks in which all support for learners with varying needs sits. It is also important to be aware that what is 'reasonable' in one setting may not be in another, and 'reasonable' in a single setting may alter with changes in staffing and cohorts, depending on the different profiles of learners. Before any specific strategies are implemented in the classroom, the main and most important support that young people can have is time. Time allows students to process and make sense of tasks, so that they can then formulate their responses to them, whether they are reading, writing or spelling tasks in literacy or activities in other curricular areas.

Name: Janie

Role: SENDCO across a small multi-academy trust

Area of focus: Safeguarding and support for young people who have literacy challenges, inspired by her own journey with severe dyslexia. Janie found literacy very challenging when she was at school and through her career has spent time focussing on supporting young people with dyslexia so that their journeys through school are smoother and emotionally easier than hers.

Ideas for support strategies:

- Young people shouldn't be expected to copy from the board – give them print outs, let them take pictures of the board, make booklets of notes for all students so that dyslexic children are not singled out.
- Discuss with young people and their families the best place for them to sit in your classroom so that they can best see the board, check in with adults in the room and move around if needed.
- Verbally plan for writing tasks; rehearse sentences orally and then use a block to represent each word so that students know how many words they wanted to write. Students can then write the words and replace the blocks as they go. This can also be done using lines on a whiteboard, sticky notes, or counters.
- Using story maps, where young people draw a pathway to represent the journey through a story. They can make notes on the story, use images and symbols to help them jot down their ideas and structure their writing.

- Allow students with different profiles to have different styles of work station. For example, some students may find sitting on the floor helps them, others may prefer a standing desk. Some students may want to sit on exercise balls or have access to a wobble cushion. Having a variety of options can be a real game-changer although what is feasible in a given setting may vary according to resources, cohorts and the logistics of classrooms.
- Don't expect children with literacy challenges to read aloud on the spot in class; they may find it very upsetting and it may impede their progress. Instead allow them to volunteer where they are comfortable to do so.
- Don't always focus on spellings in writing in the first instance; let young people get their ideas out first!
- Use a plastic overlay on a page so that young people can look through a reading passage and underline the words they know before they formally read through the passage.
- Let young people use a thesaurus to help them diversify and broaden their range of vocabulary in writing tasks. They can look up simple words that they do know and then use the synonyms for them to spice up their writing work.

Spelling Strategies

Where young people struggle with spelling, using fridge magnets or other 3D letters can relieve a substantial burden on working memory versus expecting them to write by hand. 3D, manipulable letters also provide a multisensory experience for learners who otherwise struggle to commit their spellings to memory. Using those letters to generate non-words or alien/monster names can be a fun way to support them, particularly in Lower Key Stage 2. As learners progress towards Upper Key Stage 3, they may find that rather than using letters, having access to a mini-whiteboard can be helpful for them to practice their spellings before they commit them to paper.

Young people may also find working in groups or with partners on colour coding patterns aid in their writing as they spell. This can then be reinforced by students using different media to 'write' words. They may find that forming letters on their peers' backs for example and then asking their peers what has been written may be helpful. Some students may find it helpful to use a water pistol to form letters carefully, on a wall so that they can see it in a large format. Sandboxes can also provide a multi-sensory experience for learners to develop their spelling skills

Spelling can also be supported through use of dyslexia-friendly dictionaries, where students can look up the phonetic spelling of words and find the standard spelling. This is also useful for students in Key Stage 2 as they develop their dictionary skills. Technology can be useful for young people here too, with tablet computers, electronic dictionaries and devices such as Alexa or Google Home giving students voice-activated responses to spelling questions. The implications of using these in Key Stage 2 in relation to SATS should be explored with reference to the statutory guidance for the year where the assessments are taking place.

Writing/Planning Strategies

There is no one correct way to plan, and young people in Key Stage 2 are at the start of their journey with planning strategies. It is often the case at this stage that they use planning proformas given to them by their teacher. Proformas can support young people to make use of varying strategies or formats:

- Bullet points to note down ideas chronologically.
- Spider diagrams so themes can be grouped together.
- Story boards so that young people can sequence ideas.
- Paragraph planners with sentence starters.
- Story mountains so that young people can visualise the development of their stories.
- Model answers so that young people can see where they may want to edit and make ideas their own.

However, there are other strategies such as using sticky notes to note ideas and then moving them around to organise and sequence them. Young people may also find it helpful to use Talking Tins or an equivalent resource so that their ideas are noted verbally, and they can then listen to them for prompting. Like sticky notes, using a word processor can be helpful for committing ideas to 'paper' and then using cutting/pasting to move and resequence ideas without having to restart their plans completely.

Dyslexia in Later Primary School

Reading Strategies

There are lots of different reading strategies that you can implement to support young people. If they are finding accessing passages tricky in Lower Key Stage 2, it can be helpful for them to have access to texts as part of small group interventions so they can initially work on decoding the text and cover some complex words that are implicated in the passage. That way they are not reading it 'fresh' in class; this is a way to build extra time into your students' learning without it impacting on the pace of learning in a lesson or making that extra time obvious and drawing attention to those young people who need time.

Other strategies such as paired reading, where children read alongside another individual who adapts their pace of reading to allow for complex words or changes in speed of the child. Young people may also find it helpful to have input from technology such as a reader pen, or an electronic reader where they encounter a word that they find tricky to make sense of. This will depend on what is feasible in a given setting. Audiobooks are also an exciting way for young people to engage with literature if they find reading challenging. To support them as readers and to familiarise themselves with words, young people can also follow the audiobook using a print version.

Literacy Learning Journeys

> **❓ Reflection Point: Your Classroom and Your Students**
>
> There are often small things that you can do in your practice which make some students' experiences of learning easier. This is not a long refection point, as you have had a few of those already. But take a moment here and think about students you work with who have challenges in literacy. What are those challenges and how do they manifest not only in literacy, but also in other areas of the curriculum? Are there any small tweaks you might make to their learning so that the challenges can be addressed?
>
> Is there any technology available in school to support their learning? Are there any literacy programmes online that young people can engage with independently or at home?
>
> We are going to move on to thinking about wellbeing and dyslexia, and how it can impact on young people socially. Take a moment and think about the playground around unstructured times. What may be tricky for young people with dyslexia in that instance?

Wellbeing, Dyslexia and Moving on Up

Wellbeing does transcend the Key Stages, so while it is discussed here, we also talk about ongoing support for wellbeing in Chapter 9, looking at strategies and contacts for individuals and families, as they progress through school and beyond. Young people are often reminded of the challenges they experience in relation to literacy, and this can be particularly prevalent in a Key Stage 2 classroom. Spelling tests are an arena where these differences can stand out; young people see how others have performed and may be aware of differences in outcomes. Those differences can become a sore point and young people may be singled out by others because of these challenges (Nalavany et al., 2011). Reading aloud or sharing writing outputs can also have the same effect of highlighting the challenges that young people experience and prompt them to compare themselves with others. Because of the structure of the Key Stage 2 Programme of Study for English (DfE, 2013a), where young people are expected to share their work and give/receive feedback on it from their peers, young people whose literacy is an area of challenge are at risk of adverse experiences which can link to low self-esteem and anxiety (Nalavany et al., 2011; Wilmot et al., 2023).

A large body of research highlights these links and there are suggestions of ways that young people can be supported through these challenges. Going into great detail of these strategies is outside the scope of this book. However, some suggestions in relation to supporting young people are given both in relation to their academics and also social impacts or challenges particularly with verbal processing. Challenges in verbal processing impact not only young people's ability to make sense of curricular information, but also on their capacity to engage socially with their peers. At a time where friendships are increasingly important, for young people who cannot readily 'find' the words they want to say or make sense of conversations, there is a sense of isolation and difficulty. This combined with challenges in other elements of the curriculum can make school an upsetting experience for young people.

To support young people and create a space where their wellbeing does not suffer, it is important that they feel they can be open about the challenges they experience. Giving students positive role models linked to dyslexia and other neurodiversities can be very helpful and if educators feel able to share their stories, young people can be inspired both by celebrity and 'real' people. Giving people the space and time to build positive emotions and engagement with others, so that they have good relationships which transcend difficulties, is also important (O'Brien and Guiney, 2021). That way young people can appreciate their friends and support them through the things they find challenging; if young people are empowered to share their difficulties as well as their strengths, awareness, and support, solidarity can follow. The value-culture of a setting is important here too; young people all have different skills and valuing all aspects of learners is important, even where curricular requirements may not always provide that structure. Use of cognitive behavioural strategies can be helpful to support young people but must be implemented by appropriately qualified professionals. The use of drama/role play can be helpful. Ultimately, fostering positive and compassionate relationships amongst students, celebrating their strengths and supporting them to support each other through challenges can promote cohesive and inclusive classrooms where young people's wellbeing is central.

Supporting young people holistically is vital at all stages of education. Wellbeing is linked to engagement with school and where young people have poor mental wellbeing, their ability to engage with school and the curriculum is negatively impacted. Although class teachers are not mental health professionals and should not be expected to meet young people's therapeutic needs, their input into supporting young people to develop resilience and strategies to manage their wellbeing in the face of the challenges of dyslexia is very useful. Where young people are equipped and have an understanding of their own mental health and wellbeing needs, they are better placed to move through Key Stage 2 and on towards Key Stage 3.

> Teachers often know young people the best, alongside their parents or carers. This is particularly the case in primary schools where teachers are with the same students for most of the week. That means that teachers are particularly well placed to notice changes in their students and also to support them (as part of a team) through challenging situations.
>
> As you reflect on this chapter, consider the students you work with who have dyslexia or find literacy tricky.
>
> - How to they respond to tasks?
> - Can you tweak your delivery of tasks to reduce reading or writing burdens on them?
> - Can you create a space for young people to talk about what they find hard and why? Can you support young people to share their different coping strategies with each other?
> - There is no right or wrong answer to this but it's something that is always worth considering.

Key Takeaways

- Early identification of need is vital; as young people progress through Key Stage 2, the demands placed on their literacy increase. Vulnerabilities in literacy can be a barrier to engagement with other elements of the curriculum.
- Young people do not have to write down everything; different recording methods are permissible and can immensely benefit children who have challenges in writing by hand.
- Not everyone loves reading – and that is OK! We need to be able to access the written word, but there are lots of ways in which to do that

which can minimise the reading burden on children who don't naturally gravitate towards reading as a pastime.
- Multi-sensory support is useful and helping children develop planning strategies to reduce the burden on their working memory can be a game changer for them, as they progress through towards Key Stage 3.
- The social impact of dyslexia can be substantial, particularly as children get older; friendships and relationships with their peers become more important for children and differences in communication can make these harder to navigate.
- Teachers can help build resilience in their students, as well as boosting confidence, but they should never be expected to fill the gap in mental health provision without appropriate training. Even with training such as 'Mental Health First Aid', teachers' primary function is to teach, not provide therapeutic services.

Further Reading

- For young people who are not able to access a formal assessment process for dyslexia, there are many checklists and other resources online which can be helpful in informally identifying need. This is particularly relevant given that the Special Educational Needs Code of Practice (Department for Education (DfE) and Department for Health (DfH), 2015) does not stipulate *how* needs must be identified, meaning that informal identification can play a role in developing support strategies and programmes for young people. You may find these are useful places to start when you are trying to find the best way to support your students.
- The British Dyslexia Association has a checklist for young people in primary school, which gives helpful insight into different behaviours that young people with dyslexia show when they are finding things tricky in school. You can find the check list here: https://cdn.bdadyslexia.org.uk/uploads/documents/Primary-School-Dyslexia-Checklist.docx?v=1636035265.
- Positive Dyslexia has a useful overview page where you can find information on the kind of difficulties young people may experience. This page is aimed at parents so there are questions around family history as well as academic skills. However those

family history questions may be useful to help you understand students' backgrounds. You can access the page here: https://www.positivedyslexia.co.uk/parent-and-children/. There is also a page aimed at schools, with some helpful questions roughly halfway down the page on how dyslexia may impact on young people in the classroom, which can be access here https://www.positivedyslexia.co.uk/schools/.

- The WESFORD (Wiltshire Early Screening for Dyslexia) kit is a powerful and free-to-download resource that helps build a profile of learners' needs through exploration of their phonological skills, a dyslexia checklist, various literacy assessments/tasks and working memory and sequencing tests. The kit also has a pupil profile form. It is available to download here: https://rightchoice.wiltshire.gov.uk/Pages/Download/2bda2bff-403f-4ebb-8e7b-63fe36dd8099/PageSectionDocuments.
- To help boost young people's confidence, drawing on their areas of strength is really important. It is highly likely that your students are acutely aware of the challenges they experience so supporting them to see their strengths is really important. Made by Dyslexia has a lovely interactive quiz that does just that, and it is available here: https://www.madebydyslexia.org/quiz/.

For further information about the Key Stages in England, these websites are useful and give lots of insight.

- Twinkl has a large range of resources that are helpful for families and teachers in supporting young people across the age range. There are also lots of insightful articles on supporting young people. This is an overview of the Key Stages and what the various expectations are of children at those different points of their journey through school: https://www.twinkl.co.uk/teaching-wiki/key-stages.
- This is a website aimed at teachers looking to work in London. RedBox Teachers (www.redboxteachers.co.uk) is a supply teacher agency that hosts this page. It has information about the different Key Stages and is very informative for parents and families alike, particularly relating to what is expected in English and maths: https://worldclassteachers.co.uk/teaching-key-stage-one-and-two-in-the-uk/.

References and Bibliography

Department for Education (DfE) (2013a) 'English programmes of study: key stages 1 and 2'. Available at: https://assets.publishing.service.gov.uk/media/5a7de93840f0b62305b7f8ee/PRIMARY_national_curriculum_-_English_220714.pdf.

Department for Education (DfE) (2013b) 'The national curriculum in England Key stages 1 and 2 framework document'. Available at: https://assets.publishing.service.gov.uk/media/5a81a9abe5274a2e8ab55319/PRIMARY_national_curriculum.pdf (Accessed: 21 December 2023).

Department for Education (DfE) and Department for Health (DfH) (2015) *Special Educational Needs and Disability Code of Practice: 0 to 25 Years*. London: DfE and DfH. Available at: https://assets.publishing.service.gov.uk/government/uploads/system/uploads/attachment_data/file/398815/SEND_Code_of_Practice_January_2015.pdf (Accessed: 5 August 2021).

HMSO (2010) *Equality Act 2010*. Statute Law Database. Available at: https://www.legislation.gov.uk/ukpga/2010/15/contents (Accessed: 15 February 2022).

Nalavany, B.A., Carawan, L.W. and Brown, L.J. (2011) 'Considering the role of traditional and specialist schools: do school experiences impact the emotional well-being and self-esteem of adults with dyslexia?' *British Journal of Special Education*, 38(4), pp. 191–200. https://doi.org/10.1111/j.1467-8578.2011.00523.x.

O'Brien, T. and Guiney, D. (2021) 'Wellbeing: How we make sense of it and what this means for teachers'. *Support for Learning*, 36(3), pp. 342–355. https://doi.org/10.1111/1467-9604.12366.

Tijms, J. (2004) 'Verbal memory and phonological processing in dyslexia'. *Journal of research in reading*, 27(3), pp. 300–310. https://doi.org/10.1111/j.1467-9817.2004.00233.x.

Wilmot, A. et al. (2023) 'Understanding mental health in developmental Dyslexia: A scoping review'. *International Journal of Environmental Research and Public Health*, 20(2), p. 1653. https://doi.org/10.3390/ijerph20021653.

6
Secondary School

Introduction

The importance of reading and literacy skills at GCSE level cannot be understated. GL Assessment (2023) found that 25 percent of students in Year 10 had a reading age level of age 12 or below. Given the significant correlation they also found between students' reading attainment and their eventual outcomes in GCSE examinations, there is clearly a strong emphasis on reading and all around literacy attainment in Key Stage 4, which is reflected in the work preceding it in Key Stage 3 as part of the lead-up to those crucial public examinations. It is here that students with dyslexia can be substantially disadvantaged, particularly where their needs are not identified and subsequently not addressed. This chapter talks about how young people with dyslexia may experience the impact of it in secondary school. Changes in how the curriculum works, how young people move around school and the emphasis on literacy across different structures has a substantial effect on the lived experiences of children and young people. So here, we'll walk through it and spend time reflecting on students we work with, and how we might be able to tweak lesson delivery or resource allocation to support them as well as possible within our settings.

This chapter does not provide definitive, binary responses to young people's needs. But we will take time to think and reflect on practice, consider the resources you have available to you within your settings and prompt a few thought processes that might lead to changes in your way of working as you support diverse learners with dyslexia or other literacy challenges.

> ## ❓ Reflection Point: Your Students and How You Support Them
>
> Take a moment here. We are at the start of the chapter where we will think about young people in secondary school. Secondary school is a major part of young people's journey through education, where substantial challenges may manifest and significant growth can take place. Think now about students you work with who you know have challenges in their literacy, whether formally diagnosed or otherwise. Consider these points:
>
> - What do you do to support them in class?
> - How do you reduce the burden on their literacy but still support them in accessing the curriculum?
> - What do you do differently for young people with literacy challenges?
>
> Now, consider students who may not always appear to engage in lessons. This is not about apportioning 'blame', or trying to say that teachers don't do enough; it is about seeing if there is something that you might be able to do, that could break down a barrier that your students are experiencing.
>
> - When do those students wobble?
> - Do they dodge reading or not ever seem to engage in writing tasks?
> - Could copies of notes help them and might they be able to share their understanding by talking it through rather than written work?
>
> There are no right and wrong answers to these questions. There are **your** answers in your setting, 'for now' and that may change with any given cohort as they progress through from Year 7 to Year 11 and beyond.

The Primary to Secondary Shift

Stereotypes prevail in my initial thinking of different school types. These are initial thoughts and only sit at surface level when considering different types of institutions; usually it is vital to dig deeper and I would insist on doing so. However, sometimes, taking a moment and sitting with an initial, gut feeling is actually helpful and can provide a useful starting point for careful and deliberate introspection. So, for a moment, stay with the stereotype:

- What do you think of when you think of primary school? What images come up? What kind of setting pops up in your head? The teacher? The students? The activities? How do teachers engage with their students and what does the school day look like for children?
- Now think about secondary school. How is it? What kind of work do young people do? Are the teachers different and how do they engage with their students? What does a typical day look like in the world of a Year 8 student for example? How do they move, both physically and mentally through the day?

Hold those thoughts in your mind; I imagine they are informed as much by professional knowledge and experiences as the memories you have of your own school days. All of this information – the tacit knowledge we all carry as individuals, of our own journeys through education, which we can draw on when thinking of others and their progression through school – and the experiences of our children as they work through school and our interactions with our students can all inform our responses to need and help us to create inclusive, supportive practice as part of empowering our students to thrive.

Primary school and secondary school can be very different experiences for young people, and as part of working on this book, I spoke to families about how secondary school and primary school differed. We have already addressed how dyslexia can impact on young people in primary school in previous chapters. Here the impact in secondary school is discussed but this is not possible without engaging with young people's experiences of the curriculum, subjects and their physical setting.

Everything shifts – we need to consider that so we can best support our children and young people.

Curriculum

At each stage of school, demands within the curriculum shift and how knowledge is recorded, understanding demonstrated and progress tracked seems to become more rigid and limiting. There is what seems to be an ever-increasing reliance on the written form as a way for young people to show what they have learned. Key Stage 3 subjects tend to be taught separately, with clear delineations in students' timetables for each one. English is a block on a timetable. History exists only within its timetable window and may not be linked to geography or science, which might connect learning for young people. When they enter secondary school, young people are likely to find that the cross-curricular learning they had experienced in primary school is not mirrored in their secondary setting; this is largely the case within an English context. Here it is important to note that there are substantial differences in curricula across the home nations, in how subjects are structured and learning delivered. It is important that I am clear in my professional experience and setting here too; I was trained within an English context and have worked within the English education system. I have some experience of the Curriculum for Wales frameworks via some research work that I have undertaken previously (Ross *et al.*, 2021, 2023). I don't have first-hand experience of working in the Scottish or Northern Irish contexts.

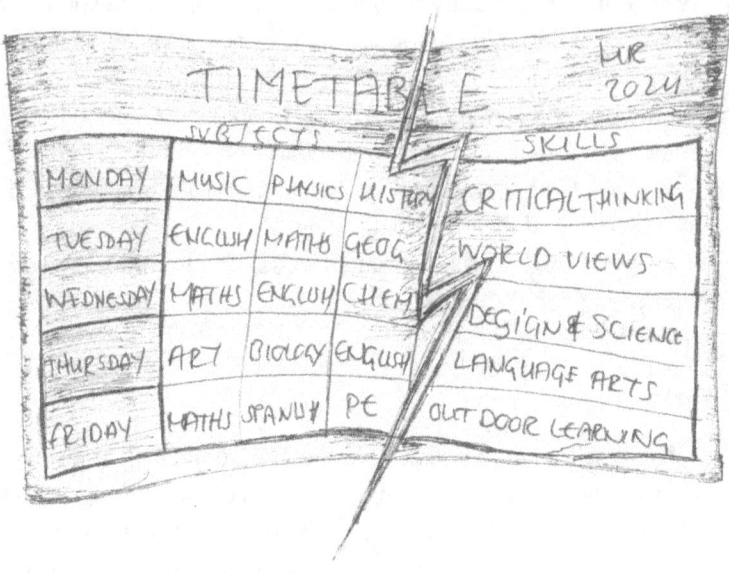

England

At present the National Curriculum for England (DfE, 2014) is divided into Key Stages, usually with Key Stages 3, 4 and 5 taking place in secondary school. Subjects have their own programmes of study which are then taken to school level and developed into schemes of work that are delivered in-house. Some schools may buy in pre-written schemes of work and other schools have in-house programmes but the common model is often located in different subjects being allocated a particular number of lessons in school timetables.

There are schools that have cross-curricular sessions for students, often at the start of Key Stage 3, as part of supporting them through transition; within these sessions, multiple subjects are taught, and young people may be within mixed groups. The physical setting is largely consistent and because more than one subject is taught at once, the sessions are often delivered in a single location in a school so that children do not have to move from room to room. Rather they stay in one setting, which mirrors their primary school experience. Although this is feasible and does take place in some settings, largely, young people move from room to room with separate subjects and different teachers in each subject. For some young people this works well but for some this can present some real challenges. However, for others the opportunity to move and refocus can be a paradigm shift. Exploring options and potential pathways forwards is key here!

Wales

Historically, the Welsh education system has been closely tied to the English system. However, recently there have been some substantial changes in the framework underpinning how schools structure and deliver learning to their students. The Curriculum for Wales (Welsh Government, Undated) grounds curriculum development in the 'four purposes' of learning which support young people to aim high and be active citizens of the world. In publishing 'Curriculum For Wales The Journey to 2022' (Education Wales, 2020), the Welsh Government set out its vision for an integrated, skills based curriculum which would be rolled out from 2022 onwards. The new curriculum is implemented at school level and subsequently may offer opportunities to vary delivery and provide flexibility where students may need it.

Northern Ireland

The Northern Ireland curriculum is spread over seven areas which mirrors elements of the Scottish system. There is an expectation that young people will develop skills relating to the three formally identified areas of cross-curricular activity, as well as other skills, such as being creative and working with others. The curriculum does not explicitly address learning 21st century skills or working with stakeholders to develop a curriculum to support learners as they approach the world of work. Structurally, Northern Ireland resembles an English context, in that young people largely take GCSEs aged 16 and progress to college subsequently to tackle A levels or vocational courses. There is a grammar school system in place and policies for SEND provision do differ but there are similarities between the Northern Irish and English systems. But, given the different cultural contexts, there may be useful insights into supporting young people with dyslexia which may be relevant in your settings.

Scotland

The Curriculum for Excellence (Education Scotland, Undated) was developed as part of the vision to support young people to develop the skills they need for working and living in the 21st century. The focus was on collaboration with stakeholders, teachers and learners, as well as their communities to develop a dynamic and flexible offer for young people. The curriculum is spread across eight broad areas rather than being broken into separate subjects, so there is an expectation of cross-curricular links being made between subjects. As I've commented above, even if you are not operating within the Scottish system, there may be some useful takeaways for you and your school in how the subjects are linked, or curricular expectations that could help support learners in your setting.

Timetable and Subjects

Curriculum impacts on timetable and subjects, but there is substantial variety for curriculum delivery and the operationalisation of the curriculum in schools, whether working in England or another of the home nations. A large sticking point for young people when they embark on their secondary school career is that of timetable. All of the 'w-words' seem to apply and it really can be overwhelming for young people, particularly where they experience vulnerabilities in executive function. The logistics of secondary school timetables versus primary school ones can be really quite tricky.

Who?

Having different teachers for different subjects can mean that young people may work with upwards of ten people each week depending on their setting. This is a substantial culture shock when compared with their previous setting and can mean that challenges students experience are not fully understood by teachers/TAs, which can lead to inconsistency in practice. Young people may find it tricky to move between and adapt to different people's ways of working, which can then impact on their ability to learn. There is a 'flipside' to this however; for some young people, having a variety of teachers means that they are not working all day, each day with an adult that they don't chime with. With the best will in the world, not every person will get along perfectly with their teacher. So in primary school, where often young people have one or two teachers for the majority of their time, if the student-teacher relationship is strained, this can be very difficult to surmount. Having a larger number of teachers offers more possibilities for positive and edifying relationships, and respite from those which are trickier to navigate.

But the potential inconsistencies for young people and the difficulties in navigating different ways of working is something that young people in secondary school are likely to need support with and should not be ignored. Consistency and reasonable adjustments to support dyslexic students are vital so that they can flourish.

What?

Different subjects at different times can be challenging and may mean that young people need to switch gear several times during the day. With a secondary timetable, there is very limited flexibility within the day for teachers and other staff members to let lessons overrun where students are taking something and running with it. Staff have to consider the constraints of the timetable and adhere to lesson changes. This is not necessarily negative but can have an impact on students, particularly if they are 'in the zone' for a subject; lesson changes can mean that they have to switch to a different topic, which can take time. There is also the consideration of different books and equipment that students need to carry with them in secondary school versus what they need in primary school. Different books need to be carryied with them often, rather than being left in a drawer across a single classroom, which can be very demanding on executive function and may be a source of stress for students who find it tricky.

When and Where?

Secondary schools tend to be larger than most primary schools and the floorplans may not always be easy to navigate. Trying to navigate to classes and find where toilets are, as well as making sure you eat lunch is not always straightforward. So for a student with dyslexia, it can be extremely challenging to navigate the physical logistics of a site when under time pressure, as well as contending with the social pressure of secondary school.

Knowing what time lessons are and where they are is difficult enough in some settings, but for individuals with dyslexia, where organisation and information processing are documented difficulties (BDA, 2010), a secondary school timetable, particularly one spread over two weeks, can be daunting. If a student has looked at the wrong day, or misread a certain element of their timetable, it can wreak havoc for them in school. They may have the wrong equipment, not be in the right place, not have all their homework, be missing PE kit and simply start everything off on the wrong foot. The subsequent effects of this, in a time-poor, high-pressure setting like a secondary school can be very detrimental to young people. Rather than focussing on learning in a lesson, they may be distracted by clock-watching, trying to remember what they have next, wondering what the best way to their next lesson is or wholly lost in the process of knowing what time it is and which lesson they are on. It is in this element of a school day that dyslexia can be all-encompassing and a substantial cause of stress.

> **? Reflection Point: Dyslexic Students in 'Big' School**
>
> Take a moment: You are 11 years old and you have just moved from a small, friendly and close-knit school where you knew everyone and everyone knew you. You couldn't move from one space in the school to another without pausing briefly to talk to a friend or smiling at an adult who knew you and asked after your parents or maybe knew if you were having a tricky time. Switch that setting for a new, imposing and probably intimidating one, where perhaps you know a few people but you don't have the same intimate knowledge of the site and there are other young people who are substantially bigger than you who may not always show their kindest side. Add to that the worry of not knowing where your next lesson is, or not being sure where the toilet is, or finding some of your new subjects just a bit tricky. The foundations of overwhelm have been laid.
>
> But they don't need to be built on.
>
> How can you switch things up for that Year 7 student? This may well need input from SLT and pastoral teams but there are some questions that you might want to consider and perhaps take back to your leadership team.
>
> - Can you show them rooms and help them get their bearings?
> - Can Year 7 students have a little wriggle room between lessons?
> - Do all students *always* need to move rooms for every lesson?
> - Is there capacity to connect subjects, move teachers around the site, and support younger students in their interactions with older members of the school community?

How?

How students learn and how lessons are delivered often changes substantially in secondary school. Different types of rooms for different classes can mean that students have several entirely different learning experiences throughout their day in school. Labs for science, workshops for DT and classrooms for other subjects all have different challenges for teachers and students alike but the common theme here is that students tend to be the ones to move around the building and they are highly unlikely in secondary school, to be able to find their way around during those first few weeks of Year 7. Even as they move through secondary school, for some children finding rooms, or dealing with carrying resources between classes remains a large worry. Their 'how' is that they can't.

 Reflection Point: Think about Your Setting

This is a short task for you and you don't need to write anything down or have huge amounts to say just yet.

This is to help you think about those stressors for young people, orking out what to do about them. Are there any crunch points in the school day that might be tricky for them? Is there any flexibility of time or perhaps a quiet space they can go to when they feel wobbly and overwhelmed?

You may not have answers for this now, but the points and ideas you have now may end up useful in due course!

Working Changes and Expectations: How We Have Lived It

The emphasis on engagement with the written word is substantial in secondary school, in ways that it might not have been previously. These two case studies show very different experiences of secondary school. One student, who was in Year 11 at the time of writing, had not had a positive experience of secondary school largely due to his challenges in literacy. Both he and his family felt that they were very misunderstood and that the school at large did not positively engage with his needs. The other student's journey into secondary school had been slightly rocky initially, but now with them starting Year 8, they are finding their experiences to be much more positive. The case studies are both taken from interviews with the families, where the students and their mums were involved. The students both spoke and engaged in the interview. Here their words are paraphrased but the themes, ideas and journeys shared are the students' own.

Name: Harry

Year: 8

Location: Home Counties

School type: Grammar School

Main challenges in school: Spelling and handwriting are really difficult for Harry. He has some vulnerabilities with his motor skills and the physical act of writing, as well as organising his ideas. Answering questions or being put on the spot in class is horrible and makes Harry feel very anxious. He has a full lesson load which includes two languages, and this can sometimes be too much, causing him worry and anxiety due to the extensive workload.

Support in place: Harry has handwriting support during registration a few times a week and is supposed to have extra time in tests, and during class activities. He has access to a laptop in some subjects and is in classes with low student numbers, which means that he feels better supported than if he was in much larger classes. Harry also has use of a fidget aide to help him channel his extra energy in class. He said that this is really helpful and he relies on it substantially. Harry and his family both feel that the strong structure and high expectations (academically and holistically) of students in the school benefit him; he is expected to be his best self and excel.

Overall experiences: Harry's experiences of secondary school in Year 7 were not ideal. Some of his teachers didn't know his needs and sadly this is still the case. Harry does not always feel listened to in school and sometimes needs support from his family to negotiate what he needs to have in class. However, Harry enjoys the variety of school and lessons are more interesting in secondary school than in primary. Harry was very anxious in primary school but now he is enjoying movement breaks that come with lesson changeovers and different subjects being in different rooms. Harry has made more friends in secondary and is finding the overall social experience of secondary school better than he did in primary. Having access to a laptop in some lessons has been a real game-changer and has meant that he has been able to get his ideas out and show his understanding without the challenges of letter formation. Harry commented that he had been completely put off English lessons when he was in primary school and since being in secondary school, he is enjoying it much more. Both Harry and his mum do feel that the SENCO in his current school is much more open to listening than when he was in primary school. Although some teachers do not fully engage with his learning profile and may not know his needs, Harry feels 'seen' by the new SENCO and much more actively enjoys going to school.

Wishlist: Harry wants to be able to use a laptop in every subject and not to have to worry about the logistics of using it. He finds using an electronic reader useful and really benefits from the spellchecker. He likes not to be put on the spot in class and wants his teachers to understand what dyslexia is properly, and how it impacts students.

Name: Oliver

Year: 11

Location: West Midlands

School type: Comprehensive – part of a Multi-Academy Trust

Main challenges academically: Oliver has substantial challenges in spelling and writing. Dyslexia was not taken seriously as a possibility for him before he was in Year 8. Spelling and writing were a little tricky for him in primary school, but dyslexia was not raised by his teachers and when suggested by his family, it was not investigated further. His teachers felt that Oliver was not working hard enough and was lazy, not bothering to check his work properly.

In Year 8, COVID-19 lockdowns meant that Oliver's mum saw firsthand the difficulties he was having and how much effort he was putting into work, and despite that effort he was still struggling to spell, organise his ideas and put his views on paper. He can write well but letter formation and spelling are substantial barriers to Oliver being able to show his knowledge and access the curriculum effectively. He and his mum pointed out that this is a real source of stress now that he is in Year 11 and his GCSEs are imminent. Science lessons are tricky and the teacher does not facilitate Oliver having access to keywords or notes prior to lessons.

Support in place: Oliver has the use of a laptop in school now, and some support to help him with managing his workload. He is able to talk with the school SENCO but other teachers are not always receptive of Oliver's diagnosis, which means that much of the support that should be in place is not. Strategies such as printed out notes, electronic copies of notes, being able to access plug sockets to charge his laptop and extra time in tasks have not been implemented in school.

Overall experiences: Oliver felt that teachers did not know about his needs and even where they did, they did not understand them. Moreover, where Oliver and his family tried to explain the impact of his dyslexia on his academic journey as well as the emotional impact of it, they were not taken seriously in school. Oliver and his mum both were comfortable talking with the school SENDCO but they felt that the level of resistance to supporting Oliver from other teachers made it very difficult for the SENDCO to be able to do their job effectively and ensure that Oliver's needs were met. Oliver feels that he has had a terrible experience of secondary school in relation to his dyslexia with resistance and not being taken seriously. Expectations of his ability were low and he was viewed as lazy, with teachers not exploring the difficulties he had any further. Although Oliver does have access to a laptop in school, there are logistical challenges when using it. The large site makes it tricky to carry it everywhere and often he is not able to charge it because of where plug sockets are located relative to his seat. Oliver (and his mum) has found that secondary school has been a battle for him, and he feels that he just needs to 'survive' it so that he can get to the next stage, and not constantly have to mask the challenges he has.

> **Wishlist:** Oliver and his mum both commented that their main priority was for teachers to be aware of the importance of 'reasonable adjustments' and to act on them. Use of a laptop or other assistive technology would be helpful so that students can take notes and progress as they need to. Oliver felt that the option to have flexible schooling would be useful, so that he could work from home or school, and not need to mask constantly. Flexibility, choice and time were key factors that Oliver felt were lacking in his secondary school but were things that would make all the difference to not only students with dyslexia, but other neurodivergent individuals.

Both students attend state schools and have had very different experiences of secondary school. Relationships and communication are salient factors that have impacted on their journeys, with both of these underpinning how well both Oliver and Harry felt supported. We have set the scene for how structures in secondary school can affect young people, before they reach the classroom. We have explored young people's journeys above. In the following section, we will talk about how dyslexia can affect students in the classroom: how their learning is impacted, how expectations are affected and broader tolls that dyslexia can take on learners in secondary school.

Dyslexia in the Mix: What Happens and Why?

Secondary school is a crucial time for young people, where they explore different social, academic and career pathways. They start to work out who they want to be and what they want to do as they progress through towards adulthood. So where children and young people have literacy challenges, there can be substantial effects on their outcomes, both socially and academically. In this section, we'll talk about the different ways dyslexia can impact on young people in secondary school.

How It Can Hit

Dyslexia does not always look like difficulties with reading and spelling, particularly in secondary school. Various definitions of dyslexia link it to challenges in organisation, motor coordination and concentration. Where young people may appear to be lazy or not putting in sufficient effort to their work, it may be that there is an underlying barrier making it hard for them. Given that up to 80 percent of young people with dyslexia leave school without formal identification of their dyslexia (British Dyslexia Association, 2019) and subsequently without the appropriate support to help them flourish, it is highly likely that a number of the students you teach or work with are experiencing substantial challenges and may not know why. The short and long-term effects of this are myriad.

Academic Difficulties

Literacy

The literacy challenges associated with dyslexia are well-documented and are relatively easy to spot (British Dyslexia Association, 2010; Wilmot *et al.*, 2023). When young people avoid reading in class, or are hesitant to do so it may be that they find it very difficult. Challenges in spelling are also linked to dyslexia and often young people with dyslexia cannot spot their mistakes, even where they have spelled the same word differently within the same piece of text. Often while I was researching this book, I found that young people had been assumed to be lazy when reminded to proof-read their work by teachers but these individuals were working incredibly hard to stay afloat academically.

Challenges in literacy impact on all other elements of the curriculum. Being able to access the written word effectively is vital in today's academic climate and for young people who find it difficult there is a substantial (and negative) impact on their attainment and subsequent life and career trajectories. GL Assessment (2023) noted the significant link between reading attainment for students in Year 10 and their subsequent academic attainment across the board. Reading attainment, spelling and handwriting can be assessed and monitored relatively easily and are often what prompts assessment of young people's needs. However, dyslexia impacts much more than literacy.

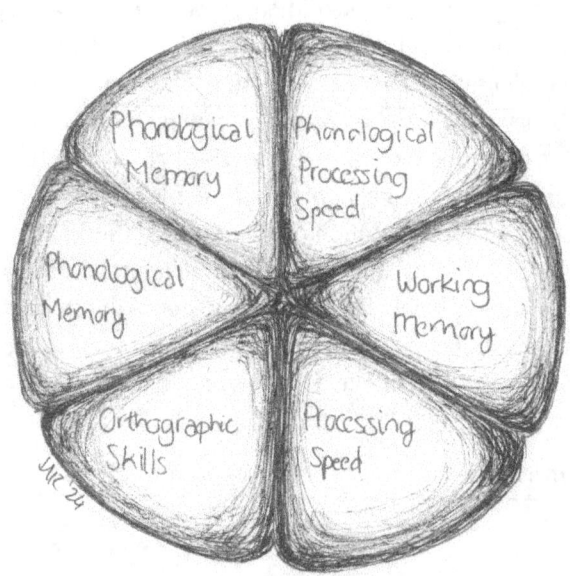

Working Memory and Processing

Working memory is a space that is hugely relied on within the education system at present. Young people are expected to tackle many problems and tasks mentally, without necessarily explicit learning of the underpinning skills to do so. Where they have vulnerabilities in working memory, doing tasks purely within working memory then becomes very challenging. The capacity to retain and manipulate information within working memory also draws on processing skills, retrieving and committing information to long-term memory. Both of these areas are implicated in dyslexia and mean that students will have trouble in performing tasks without prompts and may need to have extra time to work through them and formulate their responses.

Where students have weaknesses here, it can appear that they are not listening, or not motivated to work hard. They may 'zone out' and lose focus, not because they lack motivation rather because they are working so hard and keeping on task is a huge amount of effort for them.

Organisation

Organisation skills are linked to working memory and information processing. Knowing where to be and when, or putting ideas in a coherent order is all part of a person's organisational skills. If students seem to work hard but their schoolbooks or notes are not ordered as you would expect, or if they just cannot get their homework in on time, it may link to dyslexia. Having the right kit or learning equipment also depends on organisational skills, so although vulnerabilities in organisation skills are not a 'central' element of dyslexia, the associated weaknesses in working memory can and often do have a substantial effect on individuals.

Social Difficulties

Keeping up

The social impact of dyslexia can be substantial and is often overlooked. I would conjecture that young people compare themselves with their peers in all aspects of life; Goffman's (1963) theories on in-groups and out-groups would support that. So where they have difficulties in an element of schooling such as literacy, which can be so publicly detectable, young people will often find it difficult to keep up with others. Their reading and writing difficulties are likely to be noted by their peers; when I was researching this book, young people spoke about their classmates sometimes being unkind to them about their literacy difficulties because those difficulties were perceptible to others.

Young people also talked about the difficulties that they experienced with making sense of conversations with their friends. They found that they were still thinking about conversations or ideas that had past and had not yet been able to engage in them because of the difficulties they had in processing information or ideas. This presented them with substantial barriers to engaging with social activities at times; plans could be made and they were unaware or jokes shared and young people were just on the back foot of them. This had substantial and negative impacts on their confidence and self-esteem.

Stigma, Masking and Mental Health

Goffman (1963) found that people will usually act to hide any 'stigmatising characteristics' so that they can blend in and be accepted to the 'in-group' in any social setting. This is often the case for young people in school. The need to belong and feel part of their school community is strong and dyslexia can be a source of frustration and embarrassment for young people.

In acting to mask it, there are many different ways young people may respond. They may externalise or internalise their feelings and the challenges they have around dyslexia (Wilmot *et al.*, 2023). Externalised behaviour can look like meltdowns, or 'acting up', sometimes disrupting learning and vocally avoiding being involved in tasks. By the time they reach secondary school, young people may have become so disenfranchised with education that the challenges they have engaging with learning can mean that they spend substantial periods outside of their classroom whilst they are in school. Obviously in these instances there is a knock-on effect on students' attainment. Other students internalise their challenges so that they manifest as anxiety and a lack of self-worth (Zoccolotti *et al.*, 2016). While this may be less 'destructive' for the learning of others, internalised anxiety has a substantial effect on mental health and wellbeing, which then in turn also impacts on attainment. If you have students that seem to be quiet and 'fade' into the background when you are doing tasks that depend on literacy, it may be worth talking to their other teachers and the school SENDCO. The student may have underlying challenges and need some support.

Dyslexia in Class: What Can We Do about It?

It would be remiss to talk about dyslexia in the classroom and not to address the challenges it presents for young people, who are otherwise bright and able, to demonstrate their understanding of topics. So many assessment criteria depend on literacy and engagement with the written word, even in practical and vocational pathways, where otherwise outputs and skills monitored are practical. The implications of *not* supporting young people with dyslexia are social, academic and also have legal implications. Here we explore what we can do and the frameworks that underpin the steps to be taken.

Context: Awareness, Policy and Practice

Support for young people with dyslexia and other learning difficulties is covered by several pieces of legislation and policy documents. These set out the expectations on organisations, which include schools, and individuals when working with people with disabilities and special educational needs.

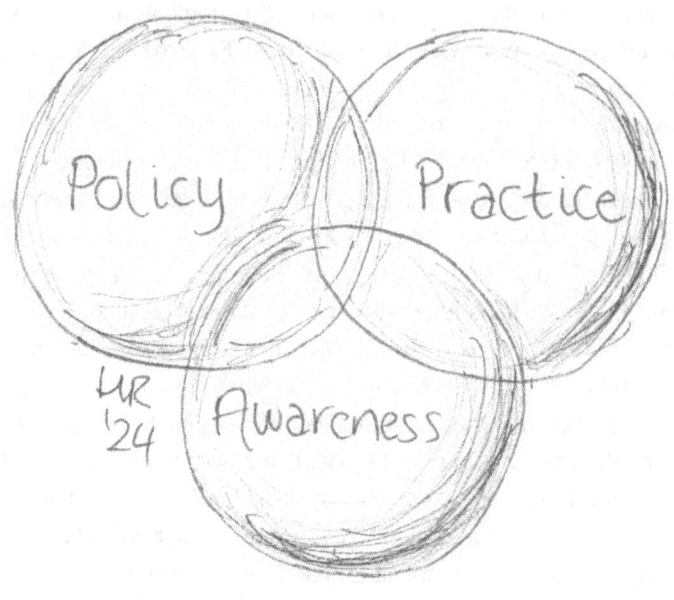

Dyslexia as Disability and Special Educational Need

Dyslexia has a substantial effect on people's ability to tackle some daily tasks and is something of long-duration which means that it can be covered by the Equality Act (HMSO, 2010). With that in mind, schools and other organisations must make 'reasonable adjustments' so that dyslexic people are not disadvantaged in accessing learning. What is reasonable varies according to institution, which can mean what is feasible in one setting may not be in another and this can be challenging to navigate. However, different schools have different cohorts and subsequently what is needed or possible within those settings varies. Dialogue with students, their families and your colleagues is vital here so that you can start to work out what is possible in your setting. Active and meaningful engagement with all stakeholders in the development of support for students is enshrined in the SEND Code of Practice (DfE and DfH, 2015). Schools are expected to work with young people and their families to develop personalised support programmes for them and monitor them regularly as part of that engagement. The type of adjustments should be carefully considered so that needs are met, young people are empowered and academic impact is trackable.

Classroom and Examination Adjustments

There are many ways in which young people can be supported in the classroom, some of which are more labour or cost intensive than other strategies you might use. How students work in class should be mirrored in how they access their examinations. For example, if a student has a word processor in class, they should have the same facility in their examinations. The Joint Council for Qualifications publishes 'Access Arrangements and Reasonable Adjustments' guidelines each year, which do change, but at the time of writing it can constitute malpractice not to allow students access to tools they use in the classroom, when they are sitting formal, public assessments/examinations. These measures do not need to be costly, invasive or prohibitively complicated to implement, however. Quick wins in the classroom include the following measures, which can be implemented quickly and effectively by teachers:

- Coloured backgrounds and dyslexia-friendly styles in their presentations. The key thing with dyslexia-friendly styles is to use sans-serif fonts and to have at least 1.5 line spacing to make it easier to read.
- Print-outs of notes are incredibly helpful. I don't think I've ever been to a conference where I am expected to copy out every slide. Usually there are printouts, electronic copies or we can take pictures and yet we expect young people to copy off the board whilst concurrently trying to make sense of what they are copying. Giving students print-outs reduces the burden on working memory and means that students can focus on content not copying.
- Electronic copies of notes can help students focus on content not copying.
- Alternative recording strategies such as presentations, drawings and discussion can be excellent and accessible ways for students' progress to be monitored. You can discern what they know without them having to rely on the written word, which can also provide vital qualitative data on students' strengths and weaknesses as part of profiling their needs.
- Extra time and warning that reading or answering questions in class may take place. Give students warning and let them know the question they

will answer in advance so that they have time to make sense of it and to formulate their response. Putting someone with dyslexia on the spot can be extremely stressful and subsequently counter-productive.
- Explicit support in developing planning strategies. Different people work and note their ideas differently so supporting all of your students to try different ways of working will give all of them a wider repertoire of tools to draw upon when working on different types of writing. For example, some students may find bullet points ideal while others use mind maps, or perhaps story boarding, or jotting ideas on a mini-whiteboard may help your students. Let them experiment in Key Stage 3, so that they have a strong grounding as they work on their GCSEs and other Key Stage 4 qualifications.

> Other strategies that you may have available in your school will likely need discussion with the SENDCO and/or leadership teams, depending on the resources available and the needs of cohorts.
>
> - Assistive technology may be useful for students. Access to word processors, or speech-to-text can be incredibly helpful for students who find the process of writing by hand very demanding. They are 'freed up' to be able to get their ideas onto paper and do not need to worry about the act of letter formation or presentation and can edit their work as needed. Some students may find that typing is challenging for them and so accessing speech-to-text packages is very useful for them; access to these does not need to be expensive, as Windows, iOS and Google have dictation as a built-in accessibility option. They also have text-to-speech, read aloud functions, which are useful in helping children access passages of text independently. There are also various reader pens that can help students to access passages of text independently.
> - Small group support can be helpful for students in various ways. The higher level of attention they receive in that setting can boost academics and also their self-esteem. Support may address literacy, study skills and/or social skills, depending on the needs of different cohorts. Phonics input could be implemented here alongside other strategies to support reading and spelling such as morphological and sight-word recognition. There is more

> flexibility of strategy in a small group and it can be good for students to have time and space to share their challenges and support strategies with other students in the same situation.
> - TA support can be helpful and meet the needs that are met by many of the technological strategies. I tend to err on the side of caution when suggesting that students work with a human reader or a scribe, because there is always the worry that students may not work independently. There are times where a person is the best way to support a student, but that is not my 'default' option.
> - Flexible/reduced timetables can be helpful for students. This does not necessarily mean that they are in school a limited number of days. It can mean that students drop an additional language, or rather than taking drama sessions they are able to go and work on their literacy in a different space or use the time to study independently and reduce their workload. It may be that students spend time at home or have specialist tuition in the spaces created by a flexible/reduced timetable; how it looks will vary according to your school, students' needs and your Local Authority/Academy Trust guidelines. These can be contentious strategies and must be very carefully grounded and monitored, equally having time and space within the school day can reap substantial benefits for young people academically and for their wellbeing.

Above and Beyond

Where young people need support that is more specialist than can be provided by mainstream classroom practitioners, there are different ways to proceed. Funding is often a limiting factor in these circumstances. Where young people's needs cannot be met within the classroom or school setting without further intervention and support, an Education, Health and Care Plan (in England – other home nations have alternative statutory documentation) may be necessary. This legal document outlines students' needs and how they should be addressed to support young people to flourish. Each Local Authority in England has differing processes for the administration of EHCPs so it is not possible to address it in detail here. Some provision detailed in EHCPs may be delivered in a mainstream school or a specialist unit linked to a mainstream school. However there may also be occasions where students' needs are complex and cannot be met fully in a mainstream setting. In those instances, which are very rare, students may find that specialist schools are the best place for them to flourish and be their best selves; detailing these types of settings is outside the focus of this book but some information on schools is available from CReSTeD, (Undated).

What's Next?

Young people may choose to stay in school or they may move onto college. The pathways following GCSEs are varied and young people's interests also vary substantially. The following chapter looks at relationships between key stakeholders in young people's journeys through education, the impact of these relationships (whether positive or negative) and some strategies to help you foster constructive dialogue as part of supporting your students. We will build on that and then in Chapter 8, we look in detail about the different pathways your students might take as they leave school.

Reflection Point: Two Stars and a Wish

Just a short thing to do here and ironically, this little job is placed under secondary school, when it is more often linked to primary schools! Here, think about your own practice as a teacher, even if you don't work in a secondary setting. Think of two things you do well to support your dyslexic students and write them down. Write them down so that they are real to you and you can't forget them, because sometimes it can be too easy to focus on what you think you do badly.

Now for the wish: think of something you would like to try when working with your dyslexic students. It doesn't have to be something you think you do badly. It can be something you would just like to tweak and do differently. Write that down and in the background, think how you might monitor whether it is helpful for your students.

Key Takeaways

- Dyslexia has a substantial impact on organisation and how young people are able to negotiate the day across various locations and a complex timetable. Verbal reminders, phone reminders, visual timetables and allowing extra time to navigate the building so students are less pressured to get everything right the first time can be really helpful!
- Use of ICT and assistive technology can be a game-changer, does not give dyslexic students an unfair advantage and is wholly permissible within JCQ guidelines. The key consideration is 'reasonable adjustments' within a school's capacity as part of their offer for students with dyslexia and other SEND.
- Not all 'reasonable adjustments' need to cost substantial amounts of money. Many can be made in the classroom by the teacher and can make a real difference to learners.
- Understanding the pressures on young people because of the structure of the day, and adjusting for that, can relieve a lot of stress and make the 'academics' of secondary school much easier.
- Time, flexibility and choice are your students' friends and can make all the difference to their journey in secondary school, and onwards.

Further Reading

To get an insight into the different ways that learning is structured in secondary schools across the UK, it may be helpful for you to look at the websites of the four home nations.

- **England:** The framework for the entire national curriculum is here, with the different subjects explained in more detail. https://assets.publishing.service.gov.uk/media/5a7db9e9e5274a5eaea65f58/Master_final_national_curriculum_28_Nov.pdf.

    There are links to the specific programmes of study for each subject area which can then be linked to schools in-house programmes. Although they are separate, there does not appear to be a formal requirement for them to be taught as such. GCSEs seem to be the driving force behind separate subjects from Key Stage 4, which then filters down to Key Stage 3.
- **Scotland**: In Scotland, the education system has remained distinct from the English system, with entirely different assessment patterns, school systems and progress monitoring. The recently developed 'Curriculum for Excellence' (https://education.gov.scot/curriculum-for-excellence/) links education to eight areas, which are broader than single subject areas but which overlap. The curriculum aims to provide flexibily and to empower learners to flourish within a flexible system. Again, even if your school is not within this system, it may be useful to explore it for ways in which you might be able to adjust the curriculum offer in your school to support young people with dyslexia and other difficulties in learning.
- **Northern Ireland:** Details of the Northern Ireland Curriculum, which was introduced in 2007, can be found here. The Curriculum covers all 12 years of compulsory schooling. https://ccea.org.uk/about/what-we-do/curriculum.
- **Wales**: There is a wealth of information on how to build cross-subject, broad and intersectional curricula on the Curriculum for Wales Hwb, which is located here https://hwb.gov.wales/curriculum-for-wales/.

    Resources to support curriculum development are shared and insight into the underpinning purpose of the curriculum is given. Even if you are not located in Wales, the resources here can provide useful guidance and inspiration if you are looking to support young people as they build links across subjects rather than focussing on siloed, individual subjects.

References and Bibliography

British Dyslexia Association (2010) *What Is Dyslexia?* British Dyslexia Association. Available at: https://www.bdadyslexia.org.uk/dyslexia/about-dyslexia/what-is-dyslexia (Accessed: 3 July 2023).

British Dyslexia Association (2019) *Educational cost of Dyslexia Report from the APPG for Dyslexia and Other SpLDs*. British Dyslexia Association. Available at: https://cdn.bdadyslexia.org.uk/uploads/documents/About/APPG/Educational-cost-of-dyslexia-APPG-for-Dyslexia-and-other-SpLDs-October-2019.pdf?v=1632303330 (Accessed: 28 October 2023).

CReSTeD (Undated) 'CReSTeD, council for the registration of schools teaching dyslexic pupils, CReSTeD'. Available at: https://crested.org.uk/ (Accessed: 28 October 2023).

Department for Education (DfE) (2014) 'National curriculum in England: English programmes of study, GOV.UK'. Available at: https://www.gov.uk/government/publications/national-curriculum-in-england-english-programmes-of-study/national-curriculum-in-england-english-programmes-of-study (Accessed: 7 July 2023).

Department for Education (DfE) and Department for Health (DfH) (2015) *Special Educational Needs and Disability Code of Practice: 0 to 25 Years*. London: DfE and DfH. Available at: https://assets.publishing.service.gov.uk/government/uploads/system/uploads/attachment_data/file/398815/SEND_Code_of_Practice_January_2015.pdf (Accessed: 5 August 2021).

Education Scotland (Undated) 'Curriculum for excellence'. Available at: https://education.gov.scot/curriculum-for-excellence/# (Accessed: 27 October 2023).

Education Wales (2020) *Curriculum for Wales The Journey to 2022*. Welsh Government. Available at: https://hwb.gov.wales/api/storage/cbe5e2c9-16cf-4eb7-87a1-c1a64fc598d8/the-journey-to-2022.pdf (Accessed: 27 October 2023).

GL Assessment (2023) 'Read all about it: Why reading is key to GCSE success'. Available at: https://reports.gl-assessment.co.uk/whyreading/images/gl-assessment-report-gcse-success.pdf?v=3.3 (Accessed: 12 March 2023).

Goffman, E. (1963) *Stigma: Notes on the Management of Spoiled Identity*. London: London : Penguin.

HMSO (2010) *Equality Act 2010*. Statute Law Database. Available at: https://www.legislation.gov.uk/ukpga/2010/15/contents (Accessed: 15 February 2022).

Ross, H. *et al.* (2021) 'How big is my carbon footprint? Understanding young people's engagement with climate change education'. *Sustainability*, 13(4), p. 1961. https://doi.org/10.3390/su13041961.

Ross, H. *et al.* (2023) 'Climate change education through the You and CO2 programme: Modelling student engagement and teacher delivery during COVID-19', *Environmental Education Research* [Preprint]. https://doi.org/10.1080/13504622.2023.2216410.

Welsh Government (Undated) 'Curriculum for wales - Hwb, curriculum for wales'. Available at: https://hwb.gov.wales/curriculum-for-wales/ (Accessed: 7 March 2022).

Wilmot, A. *et al.* (2023) 'Growing up with dyslexia: Child and parent perspectives on school struggles, self-esteem, and mental health', *Dyslexia*, 29(1), pp. 40–54. https://doi.org/10.1002/dys.1729.

Zoccolotti, P., De Jong, P.F. and Spinelli, D. (2016) 'Editorial: Understanding developmental Dyslexia: Linking perceptual and cognitive deficits to reading processes', *Frontiers in Human Neuroscience*, 10. https://doi.org/10.3389/fnhum.2016.00140.

7
Children, Teachers and Family
The Stakeholder Triad

Introduction

This chapter ties together the different elements of the earlier chapters, where the importance of positive, constructive relationships between young people, their parents/carers, and their teachers has been discussed but not fully explored and contextualised within policy frameworks.

Different interactions underpin the development of relationships between individuals and the institutions where those individuals operate. School/educational settings are no different in that respect. For example, how parents/carers and teachers can engage with each other has substantial implications for the way that institutions are able to support young people, who are the focus of those interactions. This chapter explores the interactions and relationships between young people, their educators, and their parents/carers with a view to explaining the different roles that each of these groups occupy in policy. This is done using the concept of the 'stakeholder triad', where the key voices in support provision for dyslexic children (and other SEND) are identified and their roles explained. English policy is the focus as that is my area of expertise, and where a lot of my work takes place. However, I do discuss policy frameworks in the other home nations, as often teachers and students move between the systems of the four home nations. Interactions are explored practically, through case studies and also through reflection exercises for you, as an individual working with young people to support them. Practical strategies are suggested, and you are given the space and some prompt questions as to how you could adapt those strategies to your own setting and students.

Literacy Learning Journeys

> **❓ Reflection Point: What Is the Point of School and Can Dyslexic Children Be Happy There?**
>
> Are schools and the interactions that take place there beneficial for children with dyslexia?
>
> Working with young people with dyslexia or other difficulties in literacy, a recurring theme in discourse as well as something I see in my professional practice is anxiety or stress. Young people with dyslexia are more prone to experiencing stress-related challenges or other mental health difficulties. Sometimes this is easily traceable to their experiences in school; young people compare themselves to others, are bombarded with work that seems inaccessible and they feel small.
>
> We have touched on this in previous chapters and my questions here link to the purpose of school, but also how we can support young people to flourish holistically. What is school for? Why do we send our children there and what are the outcomes we hope for them?
>
> - Thinking about what you've read from this book, and considered as you have engaged with the different reflection points and case studies, do you think dyslexic children can be happy in school?
> - If so, how? If not, why?

The Stakeholder Triad: What Is It and Who?

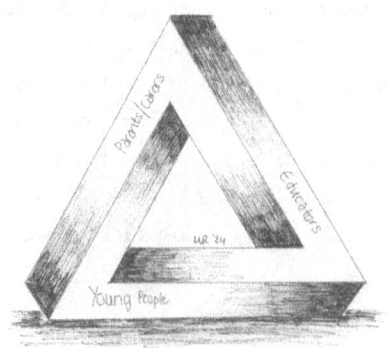

When I first went to university, I studied mechanical engineering with French. I liked hitting things and I liked maths, so for me, engineering was the obvious pathway to follow when I was 18 years old. I would get to hit stuff, then use maths to understand why it broke, so that we could make changes to stop it breaking. I did enjoy it but ultimately, I found that industry wasn't for me. I'm a people person, and interactions with others really is my bread and butter these days.

During my time doing physics and maths (which is the basis of engineering), I learnt a lot about triangles. They are the most fascinating of shapes and I promise, SOH CAH TOA (trigonometry) and Pythagoras do have real, very important uses! Essentially, triangles are the shape best suited to efficiently distribute load and support larger structures. 'Tri' or the number three, is a vital component in many physical and also social structures.

The word 'triad' captures that importance perfectly here. There are three stakeholders delineated in policy, whose input into young people's educational journey is vital: young people themselves, their parents/carers and their teachers. These three stakeholders are the 'stakeholder triad'.

Reflection Point: Positive Interactions

I imagine that you work with young people in an education setting, which is why you're reading this book. Or it may be that you're a parent/carer whose child is having a tricky time in school because of dyslexia. One thing that is true, whatever your role is in supporting a child, you want the best for them and that they flourish. What that looks like can differ substantially, depending on your perspective of the situation.

If you're looking at an elephant and standing at the front, your view is very different from someone standing at the back; this is what it can be like when making sure that children with SEND are supported. Everyone has different views of what is important, what should be in place and how it should be delivered.

This reflection point is placed here because I think that empathy and trying to understand how others perceive situations is crucial in supporting young people, whether they have SEND or not. So here, your task is to think about what positive and constructive interactions, support strategies and outcomes look like in a school. You don't need to write things down here, but the thought process involved is really important.

- What might a child/young person want?
- How might a parent/carer expect that to be supported?
- How can teachers/educators work with them to make that happen as efficiently as possible?

Policy: Key Concepts and Potential Changes

Within policy across the home nations of the UK, there are key words and concepts that are important to be aware of when exploring the different spaces that individuals and institutions occupy as stakeholders in provision for young people with any type of special educational need or disability. Already, it is important to note that I write from an English perspective, which has a huge influence on how I write, the phrases and terminology I use, as well as my perspective on different types of provision. While I do make sure that I engage with policies and practices of the other three home nations, and try to step back from the English framework – because all my teaching experience has been in that system – I do not write from a place of lived experience in the other home nations. The understanding I have of those systems is not as nuanced or deep as of that in England. That said, this book is not about me giving you definitive answers to specific questions. Rather it is about you having the information, or knowing where to find the information to help ask yourself and others the right questions. It is about you having the right words to know where to look for changes in policy, and to be able to hold your own when working within extremely complex, and sometimes very competitive systems to support dyslexic young people in your care. The following section gives you terms, policy framework and places to explore to help you do just that!

 Reflection Point: Terminology

Think about where you work, whether in the UK, or elsewhere. What are the key terms that you use every day when working with children and young people with SEND? How do they impact on your view of 'good' provision? Do you know where to look to find out more about policy and frameworks?

Are you confident in this? What might help you feel more confident?

Policy: Who Decides and Who Says So in England?

This section explores the English Special Educational Needs and Disability Code of Practice (DfE and DfH, 2015), focussing on the expectations on different individuals who are involved in supporting young people. The Code of Practice (DfE and DfH, 2015) is a large document, which talks about various different types of settings for young people between 0 and 25, so I do not discuss each type of setting here. Instead, I will use broad strokes in looking at the commonalities between settings and stakeholders across that age range, focussing on the 'triad' as described above.

Young People

The Special Educational Needs Code of Practice (DfE and DfH, 2015: 21) explicitly and unequivocally states that, 'Local authorities must ensure that children, young people and parents are provided with the information, advice and support necessary to enable them to participate in discussions and decisions about their support'. Young people's voices are centralised in processes, such that those processes are expected to be adapted and made accessible for young people with SEND, so that their voices can be heard and their views considered as part of developing their provision.

How young people are engaged in discussions does vary across ages. However, it is expected that from Year 9 (aged 13–14) onwards, discussions will gravitate towards young people's future, adult life and the steps necessary to support them towards that goal, with them living independently, and healthily. It is expected that young people are active agents in the development/implementation of support.

Parents/Carers

As with young people, the views of parents/carers are explicitly mentioned in the Code of Practice (DfE and DfH, 2015: 21). Local Authorities must have access to the information, support and advice they need to be able to participate actively and meaningfully in decisions relating to their children. Parents should have access to Parent Carer Forums, where they can liaise with other families for support, seek advice where necessary about their own children, and contribute more broadly to local provision should they wish. If young people have an Education, Health and Care Plan, parents are able to ask for a specific institution to be named for their child to attend, and also a Personal Budget to meet the costs of support in place for their children. However, it is relatively rare for young people to have an EHCP with dyslexia as the main need. In 2022–2023 (DFE, 2024), specific learning difficulties (dyslexia is not disaggregated from other needs) were noted as the primary need on 4.1 percent of EHCPs and 14.2 percent of young people with SEND Support. Therefore, it is unlikely that parents/carers will be discussing statutory provision for their children, which means they will need to have reliable and good information about what schools can do as part of their standard provision for young people.

Children, Teachers and Family

Teachers (as a Proxy for Schools)

Local Authorities are mentioned in the Code of Practice (DfE and DfH, 2015) as being responsible for provision for young people with SEND. However, in practicality, this is usually delegated to schools through SENDCOs, who coordinate provision for young people in their settings. All teachers are expected to adapt their teaching to meet the needs of young people with SEND (DfE, 2021), as part of their practice; teachers and schools are also bound by the Equality Act (HMSO, 2010), meaning they *must* make reasonable adjustments to support young people with disabilities such as dyslexia and other SEND. This means that all teachers are teachers of SEND and must participate actively in meeting needs for young people with SEND, considering their views/preferences alongside those of their families and potentially other professionals.

Reflection Point: Roles and Responsibilities in Your Setting

No one setting is the same as another but the roles and responsibilities that must be fulfilled as described in the SEND Code of Practice (DfE and DfH, 2015) do not differ across England in state-funded schools. Think about your setting and yourself within it.

- What role do you fulfil?
- How are young people consulted about their provision?
- How does your setting engage with parents in developing support for young people?

Policy: Wales, Scotland and Northern Ireland

Terminology and expectations on different stakeholders vary across the home nations of the United Kingdom. I give you a brief overview of the different policy positions here so that practitioners working in those jurisdictions have that insight.

Wales

In Wales, the terminology relating to young people with disability/learning difficulties differs from in England. Young people who may need additional support in school are noted as having 'additional learning needs' (ALN) within the Welsh Code of Practice (Welsh Government, 2021). Similarly to English policy documentation, it is expected that young people are supported appropriately to participate in processes and decision-making related to their provision. Within the Welsh policy guidelines, the 'views, wishes and feelings of the child and the child's parent' must be considered so that they can participate 'as fully as possible in decisions relating to' their provision (Welsh Government, 2021: 42). Schools are expected to identify needs, which usually will be addressed through communication between individual class teachers and 'Additional Learning Needs Coordinators' (ALNCOs). Local authorities are responsible for provision and ensuring that any statutory provision is met. As in England, the practical implementation of this is delegated to individual schools, and teachers within those settings as per the Code of Practice (Welsh Government, 2021) and the Equality Act (HMSO, 2010).

Scotland

In Scotland, young people who have challenges which make learning difficult for them come under the Additional Support for Learning Frameworks (Scottish Government, 2017). Here where young people need extra support to help them access the curriculum, they are noted as having 'additional support needs', which are expected to be met in school for the most part. Young people and their parents/cares have the right to expect that needs are identified by Local Authorities but there is a substantial difference between Scottish and other UK legislation. Within Scottish statutory guidance, specific reference is made to young people aged 12 and over having the right to actively participate in processes similarly to their parents/carers (Scottish Government, 2017: 15). However, unlike England and Wales, where no specific age limit on participation rights is cited, young people under 12 do not automatically benefit from those rights in Scotland.

As with other jurisdictions, schools and teachers are expected to implement support strategies for all young people to meet their needs, under the direction of their Education Authority. Where a 'Coordinated Support Plan' is in place, Education Authorities are responsible for providing the support detailed in it. However, the support will most likely be implemented in school (Scottish Government, 2017).

Northern Ireland

At the time of writing, there is a draft SEN Code of Practice for Northern Ireland; the previous code was written in 1998 (Department of Education of Northern Ireland, 1998), and updated by a supplement later (Department of Education of Northern Ireland, 2005). Here I will refer to the draft policy, as it is the most up-to-date model of SEN provision from the government of Northern Ireland.

As per other jurisdictions and earlier policy, young people have the right to express their views in relation to support provision, as do their parents/carers (Department of Education of Northern Ireland, 2021). How they are to be consulted is not detailed.

Although not enshrined in law at the time of writing (March 2024), the roles of both institutions and different practitioners are described in detail within the draft SEN Code of Practice (Department of Education of Northern Ireland, 2021: 31–38). Individual teachers are expected to meet the needs of their students in class, and Learning Support Coordinators liaise with professionals, within and outside of their own setting to ensure that appropriate provision is in place to meet the needs of young people in their settings.

> **Reflection Point: Practical Strategies**
>
> This reflection point links to the previous one but is now moves towards practical strategies and ways to work with others in supporting dyslexic young people in education. Think about the following points and if there are people in your school you could talk to about improving your understanding of them. If you are in a position to do so, also consider whether you might be able to develop ideas and new strategies from working with another setting to improve practice in your own place of work. In the following section, we will look at practical strategies from various perspectives, so this is a warm-up task to help you think about what is happening in your own work situation.
>
> - What is already happening in class to support young people?
> - What can be done in class to support young people without adding substantial work onto professionals' workloads?
> - How might you be able to share practice between home and school?

The Stakeholder Triad: Practical Examples and Approaches

This section gives examples on how to work with different stakeholders and takes examples shared in interviews carried out for this book. I also draw on my own professional and research experiences to share some ideas of how to work collaboratively and effectively to support young people you work with or support. The examples are given in the context of the 'stakeholder triad' and are practical, to help you develop ideas for how to work with others in your setting.

Children's Voice

Harry and Jenny had a really difficult time, particularly in primary school. His views were not listened to, and the concerns raised by Harry's mum went unheard by the SENDCO. One factor that supported Harry was to have his views actively sought, acted upon and fully considered. Where possible his needs were addressed and he subsequently flourished. No setting is perfect and there is always progress to be made in supporting any learner but Harry's secondary school seemed to 'get it' in a way that his primary school did not. Below we share little bit about his journey through to Year 8, with a case study for you to consider in your own setting.

Harry and School

Primary school – what went wrong:
In primary school, Harry's family talked through the challenges he experienced with his teachers. He was asked what he found difficult (phonics). Harry found it very tricky to break words down phonologically; he prefers to use other strategies such as sight words or morphological approaches. He told teachers that he found phonics difficult but interventions he worked with focussed solely on this and did not tap into other skills he had for manipulating language. He felt frustrated, which left him feeling very low and disenfranchised with school.

Harry's views and what he wanted:
Harry was able to work well with sight words, morphology and found using 3D letters was also helpful as it bypassed him needing to worry about letter formation whilst thinking about spellings. He didn't want to do more phonics intervention as it was very upsetting for him. Harry wanted to be able to use a laptop for extended writing tasks, so that he could just get his ideas out and not worry about letter shape or spelling until he had put all his thoughts and ideas onto paper.

Secondary school and some successes:
When he arrived at secondary school, Harry's teachers were aware of the challenges he had in spelling. The SENDCO had read his file and spoke to him about the type of support he might want in place. Harry said that he would find a laptop helpful and that dropping a language would be helpful for him too. He was given access to a laptop, which has been fantastic for him in history, in particular. Harry is still doing French at the moment, because having a laptop has made other subjects easier, so his progress will be reviewed to see whether he still feels doing French is too much for him. He is happier. He feels more at ease, has a broader group of friends and is much less tired than at primary school, largely due to his views being valued at secondary school.

❓ Reflection Point: Supporting Students in Your Own Setting

Think of students you work with. Is there anyone who has dyslexia or who may have some literacy challenges that have not been formally identified (diagnostic assessments for dyslexia can be difficult to obtain)? Think about how you meet their need and whether their written outputs match up to their verbal responses. In the first instance, talk to the SENDCO (or equivalent) in your setting to see if there may be anything you can do to support them within 'reasonable' measures for your setting. Important here, is making sure that you communicate with the student concerned and their parents/carers where appropriate; this is why it is vital to talk to the SENDCO, as there may be factors at play you are not aware of. Think about:

- Text in passages: font, spacing, background colour on board, paper colour.
- Recording of notes: copying from board, typed paper-based copies, electronic access.
- Assessment of learning: does it need to be written prose, presentations, pictorial, modelled.

Most of these elements are easy tweaks to delivery but if you have students who have dyslexia, talk to them sensitively and without drawing attention to them, to see what their preferences are within the reasonable changes you can make to lesson delivery. Then act on those discussions. Check in with students and see if things are easier for them. Little chats and small changes can make a huge difference to children's experiences of school.

Parents' and Carers' Voice

Natasha's journey in school was complex and at times, very upsetting – she is dyslexic – so when her daughter Jessica seemed to be having some of the same difficulties that she experienced, Natasha contacted the school. Reading, processing questions and responding to them under time pressure were very tricky for Natasha and also Jessica. The major concern she had was that Jessica was in Year 11 and her GCSEs were imminent. Having had no access arrangements herself in Year 11, Natasha wanted to make sure that Jessica had the opportunities that she did not. Natasha wrote to the school, whose SENDCO then followed up with a phone call to make sure they had understood what Jessica was finding difficult.

Jessica was assessed for access arrangements very quickly in school, and was granted extra time, a reader and a scribe for her GCSEs. The school did warn Natasha that Jessica's progress and trajectory would likely mean she would need to retake maths and English. However, Jessica's results were outstanding and she passed both maths and English at higher than a grade 4, having made use of all the access arrangements that she had in place. By listening to Natasha's concerns about Jessica's progress, and then acting on them, the school made adjustments to Jessica's exam delivery, which she and Natasha feel directly contributed to Jessica's success at GCSE.

The school processes were streamlined and efficient, which enabled the family's concerns to be heard and changes to be made in school to Jessica's benefit. The short reflection point below will help you to focus on your setting and how families' views are sought and acted on there.

> **? Reflection Point: Families and Carers**
>
> Young people's families and carers often know them better than anyone else, which means that they can offer huge insight into their strengths or difficulties. Think about your setting and the role you have there:
>
> - How do you know what families think?
> - What policies are in place to help families link with the relevant staff in school, so they can share their views?
> - How do families know what is done after they have shared their views?
> - Are there any steps you could take to improve any of the above?

Educators' Voice

There is no single voice of an educator within SEND systems. Various individuals often work with young people who have dyslexia as they progress through school; within English national policy only the role of the SENDCO is formally identified in policy (DfE and DfH, 2015). When considering how teachers' views are captured and considered in your setting, it may be useful to refer to the draft Northern Irish policy guidance (Department of Education of Northern Ireland, 2021: 31–38), as the different roles of teachers, including their responsibilities and rights with in SEN framework are explained. This could be helpful for you in deciding how teachers' and other educators'/professionals' views are included in discussion, particularly where support does not fall within statutory provision.

Class teachers, SENDCOs, teaching assistants and pastoral support professionals all have different insights into working with young people; it is like looking at an elephant from different angles and each person's

Children, Teachers and Family

perspective is different but not wrong. There are many different ways that views can be sought and considered, some of which do not take substantial effort to gather but can change the experience of young people.

 Reflection Point: Educators' Views

More often than not, dyslexic children's support interventions fall within non-statutory frameworks, so it may be trickier for all those working with children to share their views on supporting them. Think about your setting:

- What is in place in your school that allows teachers to share their views on how young people with dyslexia are supported?
- Have you been able to discuss support strategies for dyslexic young people you work with, particularly when considering how to meet their needs in class?
- How confident are you with your school's usual ways of supporting dyslexic children, and are you able to adapt everything you need to within that framework?
- Are you consulted on in-school policy changes?

Teachers – considering their views badly and better:

Natalie had worked as a Specialist Dyslexia Teacher across a few schools since COVID-19 closures. She is highly experienced and is not afraid to speak her mind. However, before working independently, as a freelance consultant, Natalie had some very challenging experiences because her expertise and subsequent professional opinions clashed with management decisions in her settings. What her students needed for support did not align with school management views.

Student needs

Natalie worked with students for whom phonics instruction had been disastrous. She was in a secondary school, working with young people aged 11–14, whose literacy and engagement with school was very precarious. She saw that they needed a different approach to their literacy and voiced this in school.

School decisions

The leadership in Natalie's school was only prepared to support her working with students using intervention packages grounded in phonics. They were not prepared to allow her to deviate from pre-defined schemes of work, despite her being able to show progress through this when reviewing young people's progress periodically. Her views as a professional were not taken into account when she was working with young people.

Natalie's pathway forwards

Natalie chose to develop her own scheme of work for young people which used a morphological and sight words-based approach. However, to do this she had to leave her post, which meant that young people lost the benefit of her innovative approach and her professional expertise. Students' IEPs lost the input which gave them strategies to help dyslexic individuals make progress, which ultimately was detrimental to the school as others could not read her ideas and be inspired.

Agency and Power in Support: Concluding Thoughts on the Stakeholder Triad

Across the home nations, meeting the needs of young people with dyslexia is a complex process. As a 'learning need' dyslexia is rarely subject to statutory provision, such as an EHCP in England. This can mean that the resources to meet the needs of young people with dyslexia are scarce; funding is unlikely to be ring-fenced and tight budgets can mean that children with non-statutory provision for the SEND are not prioritised in school. However, there are many tweaks to provision that can be made quickly, relatively cheaply and easily in settings without substantially increasing teacher workload, or singling out young children/young people because of their needs.

The details of the support frameworks for young people with SEND do differ across the home nations in their detail, and the type of participatory rights for young people have. However, wherever young people are based, a resounding theme within my own professional experience, within research literature, and in the research I did for this book has been choice and empowerment for young people and their families. In settings where young people's perspectives of their learning are not considered, their wellbeing suffers and subsequently their engagement can also be negatively impacted. If parents are not actively engaged and their input valued in processes, where needs are identified, fostering constructive and edifying relationships can be very challenging. Conversely, where young people and their families feel that their views are meaningfully listened to and considered, young people are able to make progress, their holistic situation improves and they are at ease. This impacts on their academic attainment, friendships and overall wellbeing. Parents and carers describe similar experiences. Where schools work with them to identify need and support young people, families are better able to engage in decision-making processes because they feel their views are valued.

A key tenant of the Code of Practice (DfE and DfH, 2015) within English policy is that young people are supported, their views considered and support measures to meet their needs should prepare them for independent life, as they move towards adulthood. The best way to do this is to listen to their views and act on them where possible, and where it is not possible, communicate carefully and sensitively why this is the case with young people and their families.

Key Takeaways

- Schools in England must consider the views of young people and their parents/carers in all decision making. How this happens will likely differ across educational settings, age groups and regionally.
- Communication is key. Where educators and by proxy, education settings, keep families and young people up-to-date about provision, listen meaningfully and act on feedback from young people and their parents/carers, positive relationships are more readily fostered.
- What different schools can manage differs, depending on their resources, staffing and individual children's needs/preferences. There is no one-size-fits-all approach.
- The 'triad of stakeholders' is only as strong as the 'weakest' connecting element. Relationships are those connecting elements. If relationships

are not constructive, honest and open, then challenges may lie ahead in ensuring young people are appropriately supported. This can sometimes mean that schools say no to things that are not feasible; it can mean that families do not want certain types of support; it can also mean that young people do not want a particular type of intervention or support strategy that others may have suggested for them. For the triad to work effectively and be a cohesive force for the benefit of young people, all stakeholders need to be able to say 'no' sometimes, or ask difficult questions of each other.

Further Reading

- Although this is aimed at parents, there are some excellent resources on this page of the British Dyslexia Association, which may help you develop strategies for supporting young people in your setting: https://www.bdadyslexia.org.uk/advice/children/my-childs-education/reasonable-adjustments-in-education (Accessed 29 March 2024).
- Louise Selby has some fantastic resources aimed at schools for supporting young people with dyslexia in school. She runs courses and has written books on supporting young people in school. Her website is available here: https://louiseselbydyslexia.com/about-louise-selby-dyslexia-specialist/ (Accessed 29 March 2024).
- I wrote this book chapter, 'It's a Battle!: Parenting and Supporting a Child with Dyslexia' following my PhD and it describes parental experiences of engaging with their children's school. It is academic in style but freely available here: https://www.intechopen.com/chapters/73999 (Accessed 29 March 2024).
- It is worth looking at the different Codes of Practice in place in your area, so that you have a clear understanding of the roles, responsibilities and rights of different stakeholders. They may change over time, as policies are updated, so regularly revisiting them is a good idea from a professional development perspective.

References and Bibliography

Department for Education (DfE) (2021) *Teachers' Standards*, p. 15. Available at: https://assets.publishing.service.gov.uk/media/61b73d6c8fa8f50384489c9a/Teachers__Standards_Dec_2021.pdf (Accessed: 30 March 2024).

Department for Education (DFE) (2024) 'Create your own tables, 2022-2023 data'. Available at: https://explore-education-statistics.service.gov.uk/data-tables/special-educational-needs-in-england/2022-23?subjectId=8853ca31-33aa-46b3-9638-08db70394ab1 (Accessed: 29 March 2024).

Department for Education (DfE) and Department for Health (DfH) (2015) *Special Educational Needs and Disability Code of Practice: 0 to 25 Years*. London: DfE and DfH. Available at: https://assets.publishing.service.gov.uk/government/uploads/system/uploads/attachment_data/file/398815/SEND_Code_of_Practice_January_2015.pdf (Accessed: 5 August 2021).

Department of Education of Northern Ireland (1998) 'Code of practice on the identification and assessment of special educational needs'. Available at: https://www.education-ni.gov.uk/sites/default/files/publications/de/the-code-of-practice.pdf (Accessed: 29 March 2024).

Department of Education of Northern Ireland (2005) 'Supplement to the code of practice on the identification and assessment of special educational needs'. Available at: https://www.education-ni.gov.uk/sites/default/files/publications/de/supplement.pdf (Accessed: 29 March 2024).

Department of Education of Northern Ireland (2021) 'The draft code - Section 2 - The law, roles, rights and responsibilities_0.pdf'. Available at: https://www.education-ni.gov.uk/sites/default/files/consultations/education/The%20draft%20Code%20-%20Section%202%20-%20The%20Law%2C%20Roles%2C%20Rights%20and%20Responsibilities_0.PDF (Accessed: 29 March 2024).

HMSO (2010) *Equality Act 2010*. Statute Law Database. Available at: https://www.legislation.gov.uk/ukpga/2010/15/contents (Accessed: 15 February 2022).

Scottish Government (2017) 'Supporting children's learning: Statutory guidance on the education (additional support for learning) scotland act 2004 (as amended): Code of practice (third edition) 2017'. Available at: https://www.gov.scot/binaries/content/documents/govscot/publications/advice-and-guidance/2017/12/supporting-childrens-learning-statutory-guidance-education-additional-support-learning-scotland/documents/00529411-pdf/00529411-pdf/govscot%3Adocument/00529411.pdf (Accessed: 29 March 2024).

Welsh Government (2021) 'The additional learning needs code for wales 2021'. Available at: https://www.gov.wales/sites/default/files/publications/2024-01/220622-the-additional-learning-needs-code-for-wales-2021.pdf (Accessed: 29 March 2024).

8
Life After School

Introduction

The pathway forward for students once they finish school can be very complex and young people have a variety of different options, whether they finish school-based learning at 16 or 18. They may wish to pursue on-the-job training, a more traditional academic route, or have their own vision as to how they will move forwards once they have finished formalised compulsory learning. This chapter shares ways that young people's dyslexia may influence their decisions after school and how different pathways relate to each other. Case studies of different people whose journeys are very different are also shared, so that you can help young people to forge their own pathways.

A Bit of Background: Life Beyond School

Dyslexia can impact academic outcomes, mental health and overall life trajectories (Nalavany et al., 2011; Antonelli et al., 2014; Alexander-Passe, 2023). Identification of need and gaining a full understanding of their own profile is vital for learners. We have already seen in this book the importance of young people and those supporting them having an in-depth understanding of their needs at school. However, the need for understanding and awareness of dyslexia does not stop when young people leave school and move onto the next stages of their lives. Under the Equality Act (HMSO, 2010), dyslexia is classified as a disability; its effects persist and can negatively and substantially impact on individuals' daily lives.

As educators, this means that we need to equip our learners with the life skills to support them moving into work, higher education and adulthood. This is expected within the SEND Code of Practice (DfE and DfH, 2015), but it is also the right thing to do! School is not the end of the journey for dyslexics (or anyone for that matter!). It sets us along our way and so often the support, skills and relationships we foster there provide a formative foundation for our subsequent trajectories. This chapter shares the stories of some adults, linking to their experiences of school and what they have done since. I will talk through practical strategies and I give an overview of legal foundations relevant to the workplace and post-school settings. This book is about supporting children and young people to flourish, so helping equip them should include both pragmatic support strategies and understanding of legal frameworks in place to protect them too.

What Can We Do

I wholly believe that there is no single, objective definition of 'success'. Some conceptualisations of 'success' link to students attending university; schools and colleges are being monitored on the pathways that their students follow after completing their studies with progression to university or other higher education settings as a specific focus of the Department for Education since 2019 (DfE, 2020). This puts pressure on schools and subsequently students to pursue an academic pathway, even where it is not right for them. It is important to help students reflect on what they want to do during the final stages of their schooling, to make sure they can make informed choices, and are fully supported in that process. Individuals have different journeys, and they define *their* success differently.

Here, I will share a few success stories with you. These are people in the public eye, and whose journeys can be followed online. Their pathways after school vary, but they are each well-known in their fields. Their journeys are 'out there', but here are the key points and highlights of their experiences.

Name: Dr Maggie Aderin-Pocock MBE

Current occupation: Researcher and scientist; science communicator and TV presenter

Early life: Dr Maggie grew up in London, spending some of her younger years in Camden. Dr Maggie's middle name (Ebunoluwa) means 'gift from God' in Yoruba; her parents were originally from Nigeria. Dr Maggie moved around a lot when she was a child, and had attended 13 schools before the age of 18. Dr Maggie really liked the Clangers (a TV show) when she was little and felt inspired by it to become an astronomer.

School experiences: Dr Maggie found out she was dyslexic when she was eight years old and this affected her journey through school. She went to a Catholic comprehensive in North London where a teacher suggested that nursing may be good for her to pursue when she said that she was interested in astronomy. Dr Maggie overcame many challenges in her personal life, including her parents breaking up, and achieved A levels in maths, physics, chemistry and biology, despite finding school challenging at times and not always being able to get her ideas down on paper.

Life after school and work: Dr Maggie was very academic in school and decided that she wanted to follow a pathway that took her to university. When she finished school, Dr Maggie decided she wanted to study physics, so she went to Imperial College London and gained her BSc. She later went on to do a PhD in Mechanical Engineering there too. After finishing her PhD, Dr Maggie worked for the UK Ministry of Defence on various projects. Then, she went back to Imperial College to develop some specialised technology for the Gemini Telescope in Chile.

She has subsequently worked a range of projects and set up a science communication company, where she has worked with more than 300,000 school children to inspire them to follow careers in science. She is a presenter on The Sky at Night and consults for a lot of other TV shows. Dr Maggie is now Chancellor of Leicester University and regularly shares her experiences of being dyslexic both at school and in the workplace.

Further information:

- You can look at her work with the BBC online: https://www.bbc.co.uk/programmes/profiles/3trm0Y2037DNmqMyjm5gQvS/dr-maggie-aderin-pocock.

Name: Jamie Oliver MBE

Current occupation: Jamie is a chef, restaurateur and author.

Early life: Jamie is from Essex and has one sister. His parents owned a pub/restaurant and Jamie used to spend time in the kitchen when he was younger, practising his cooking.

School experiences: Jamie went to school locally but did not have an easy experience. He was in special educational needs classes for a lot of time when he was at school and was not always able to participate in mainstream classes with his peers. Jamie has said in the media that he didn't feel supported in school with his dyslexia, even suggesting that it was not recognised at all. He did not have appropriate support and left school with two GCSEs in art and geology.

Life after school and work: Jamie's pathway after school was not a traditionally academic pathway. Instead, he went to college and did a qualification in home economics, which built on the experiences he had from working with his parents in their pub. His first 'proper' job working in a kitchen was as a pastry chef working in Antonio Carluccio's restaurant. That was the start of his passion for Italian food.

Subsequently, Jamie's career has seen him open restaurants, release TV series, write books and work with the government to improve school-dinner provision for young people in schools both in the UK and the US. Interestingly, Jamie has said that he read his first book in full at the age of 38.

Further information:

- For information on all of Jamie's projects, have a look at his website: https://www.jamieoliver.com/.
- There is a video of him talking about his dyslexia here: https://www.bbc.co.uk/news/av/uk-65264367.

Name: Steven Bartlett

Current occupation: Investor and entrepreneur

Early life: Steven's mum is from Nigeria and his dad is English. He was born in Botswana but when he was two years old, his family moved to Plymouth and he went to school in the city. His mum doesn't read or write but his dad is a structural engineer.

School experiences: Steven did not find school an easy experience. He was aware from a young age that if he wanted to have anything, it would be on him to find a way to earn money to have it. He found school challenging and did not always flourish academically, often feeling insecure. However, he did start to develop his head for business there, even winning contracts with vending machine companies.

Life after school and work: Steven did pass his GCSEs and A Levels, and started a course in Business Management at Manchester Metropolitan University. However, he chose to leave the course after attending a lecture and deciding that it wasn't what he wanted to do, and wasn't the way that he would achieve his goals. On leaving university, Steven set up a marketing agency which is now valued at more than £7 million. He is also on Dragon's Den and is the youngest investor yet! He hears others' pitches and invests in their companies to help them realise their dreams. Steven says that his dyslexia has never held him back!

Further information:

- Steven's website is here and gives you lots of information about his current projects: https://stevenbartlett.com/.
- His profile from Dragon's Den on BBC is here: https://www.bbc.co.uk/programmes/profiles/58CRTt8GKmQk3PqbQzYTJTM/steven-bartlett.

Name: Paloma Faith

Current occupation: Singer and actress at present, having formerly been a dancer. TV presenter.

Early life: Paloma was born in London. Her mum is English and her dad is Spanish, but they both grew up in Norfolk. Paloma danced when she was younger, doing ballet alongside more modern types of dance.

School experiences: Paloma went to mainstream school and did her A levels at college in Central London. She has been reported as saying that she finds numbers tricky but also that she is dyslexic too. After college, she decided to go to dance school. She did find elements of school tricky but, as a child, Paloma did enjoy books.

Life after school and work: Paloma initially pursued a career as a hip hop dancer and then studied at Central St Martin's College. She then moved into music and is now known for being a singer with a lively voice. She is influenced by jazz and has a retro style. She has not followed a traditional academic pathway, but has a really varied career.

She has helped to raise awareness around dyslexia, and recently encouraged children to take part in the BBC's '500 Words', a short-story competition. Paloma has also spoken about the impact of dyslexia on her wellbeing, commenting that she often felt that she was not good enough when she was younger.

Further information:

- You can read about Paloma's experiences here: https://www.independent.ie/entertainment/music/music-news/paloma-faith-i-always-feel-that-im-not-good-enough/30381777.html.
- Paloma's website is here and gives you lots of information about her career at present: https://www.palomafaith.com/.
- A snippet of information on Paloma's dyslexia is here: https://www.womenshealthmag.com/uk/health/g38640983/celebs-with-dyslexia/.

Life After School

It can be really inspiring for students to see the different pathways of other dyslexics, and their successes. However, it can be tricky for young people to relate to the experiences of rich, famous and prominent people in their lives. Sometimes, it is helpful to share more common, 'regular' pathways so that students can draw parallels with their own lives and envisage how *they* might follow in someone's footsteps.

Post-compulsory Pathways

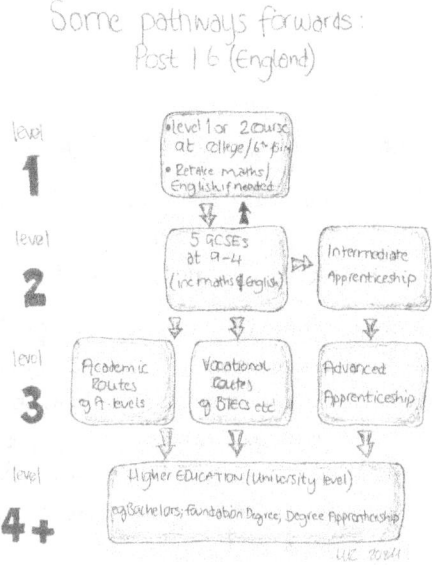

Choosing what to do, even for GCSEs, can be a very daunting prospect for young people so when they are faced with the transition out of compulsory schooling into a freer, more flexible pathway, it can be very difficult. At 18, or even 16, for young people who don't want to stay in 'school', choosing what comes next is a huge task. They need to be able to explore potential avenues that exist, think about what they like or are good at, as well as what they don't like. Once they have figured that out, young people then need to

Literacy Learning Journeys

try to marry together their strengths and weaknesses with courses, jobs and training routes that are available in their area. This is the 'best' case scenario, where other factors such as caring responsibilities at home, transport limitations, financial constraints within their families and social pressure, don't influence their choices. With the addition of these other pressures, choosing a pathway forward may seem impossible.

As educators, it's our job to help students to see their strengths and support them in linking them to the next stage of their journey, whether they are in Year 2, thinking about whether to try for the netball team, or in Year 13 and deciding if they want to do a degree-apprenticeship or to join the army.

What's your name: Jake

Current occupation: Widening Participation Officer in HE

When did you find out you were dyslexic: I think it's probably like the April of my final year of uni… I think for a long time they had been like this or like feeling that something wasn't necessarily right.

What was your journey through school like? My primary school was really good without formalising it so that I used to leave certain lessons and do like extra English but again, never with that sort of 'dyslexia' tag. It was just that, you know, 'Jake struggles'. There's about six of us that were taken out of a certain lesson, which I can't remember what it was. But we would go like weekly and have like a separate session. I always, I was always that sort of, 'he's getting Cs' sort of student, I think. And I think that support hadn't necessarily transitioned into secondary school that well. Not behaviour-wise or socially, like I was always like, did have friends and stuff. But in terms of like my development, and my Year 6 SATs I think I got all 5s, no 4s in English. But then for my Year 9, I think I'd gone up in maths, maths and English, but science just stayed stagnant. And what was happening with science was I always thought that science was a really interesting lesson. But because of what used to happen all the time was, the class would take the teacher about 25 minutes, for them to get the class settled. And then they would try and cram in an hour's worth of work in but they'd lost 25 minutes. Those go really fast pace, which I'm okay at sort of like this. But then we would be asked to like write what we're doing in the books. And that's the bit that I couldn't do fast enough. I just can't write it down. So I remember those moments. And I also just remember like, being like the last, we used to have in primary school we used to have like pencil writers and handwriting.

What did you do next? I went, went to college and did a BTEC in sport, which was a really interesting choice in itself because your, your I think, by the type of work that I do now, I start to realize how much how wrong I might have been about my abilities basically and my skills and qualities. I had the idea that I should choose sport, because that's where I saw a version of the successful me. I stayed at my local college for the first two years then I went to University.

Playing to Your Strengths and Likes after School: Freedom

We often hear the phrase 'play to your strengths' and I have definitely used it a lot with my students. However, I'm not sure that I've always helped young people play to their strengths as effectively as I might have done. Dyslexia has many benefits and sometimes this can get forgotten. People like Kate Griggs (2018) have undertaken a lot of work around the strengths inherent in dyslexia. Other work has also highlighted the importance of recognizing the strengths of dyslexia so that individuals can thrive (Kannangara et al., 2018).

Communication skills may be an area of strength for dyslexics. Dyslexic people think outside of the box and see the 'bigger picture', and importantly *communicate it* to others in ways that 'neurotypical' individuals cannot. They are creative and can express themselves well, visually and verbally (Antonelli et al., 2014; Griggs, 2018). As students move on from compulsory education, their creative and innovative problem-solving skills will be invaluable. Flexibility of thinking, reasoning skills and good spatial awareness are skills of dyslexic individuals. Dyslexic young people often have strengths in their social abilities; empathy and resilience underpin strong emotional intelligence which are the foundation of people management skills (Antonelli et al., 2014; Griggs, 2018; O'Brien and Guiney, 2021).

These strengths are relevant to different pathways but young people may have spent so much time being assessed and evaluated in ways that don't allow them to shine, that they have forgotten what they're good at. As educators, we need to remind young people of their strengths, help them recognise them, and channel them constructively.

Academic

Sadly, many people I work with have had awful experiences along their pathways through school and beyond. They often say that their schools viewed them as unintelligent or lazy. Academic pathways can feel out of reach to young people with dyslexia. This is often linked to their challenges in showing their ideas or knowledge of a topic via the written word. But this doesn't mean that they don't understand something. It just means that they need to work differently to share their thoughts. There are many ways to approach academic pathways and I think it is really important for dyslexic people to remember that although academic routes do 'finish' with a degree, the way there is not always linear and can be very exciting!

The traditional 'GCSE-> A Level-> Gap Year (maybe)-> University' pathway may be perfect for some people but for others it may feel foreboding or quite simply may just seem a bit boring! As educators we should help young people to see different possibilities and decide which way is best for them.

A-levels, Highers or other Courses?

The 'Prospects' website has existed since I was a nipper (my A Levels survived the Millenium Bug, as an indicator!). There is a wealth of information on various post-16 pathways for young people. The website does promote a traditional pathway towards university as the most popular option if students want to go to university (Higginbotham, 2022). While this may be what your students want, you need to make sure that they are fully informed of other options if they do not take A levels, but still want to go to university. Many students take other courses such as apprenticeships and International Baccalaureate, as well as Access Courses.

What's your name: Isabella

Current occupation: Record Manager and Administrator

When did you find out you were dyslexic: So, I got tested when I was in primary school. That was about eight or nine, and borderline. Then they said ok and get tested when you go to secondary school. And then I think the primary school talked to the secondary school saying, 'She's got, she's borderline dyslexic'.

What was your journey through school like: I was just put back in English and she [the SENDCO] thought like I was stupid. And so I was out and it didn't help that the teacher, you know the SENDCO, yeah, the SENDCO didn't believe in dyslexia. My mum had arguments with her. Yeah, apparently she didn't believe that dyslexia was such a big thing. I think I had like some interventions and changes. Like, I know that in Year 9, I was allowed to not take German so I could do extra English lessons, which was just basically a computer program teaching me how to touch type.

Then, I went away to school in Australia for a year and again was like 'borderline dyslexic'. I had some lessons there. But the difference was they don't set their English class. They don't 'set' [group by ability] in English. So suddenly I started doing a lot better in English. I got an A in something. And I really enjoyed English all of a sudden! We're doing books! We're doing amazing work! And then I had to go back. So, I came back midway through Year 11, midway through

> my GCSEs. So, when I was in Australia, my mum paid for me to get a tutor so that I could actually study what I was missing in my GCSE. So that when I came back, I'd learned all of the stuff that was in my English literature GCSE. And then I got told, 'Oh, yeah, but the "bottoms" don't do the literature'. And they didn't let me do the literature. And my mum had to pay privately for me to do English literature.
>
> I like writing. I like studying books. And just to be told that, 'You don't do that. You're not clever enough. Or that's too clever for you'. It's just like, I'd come back from a teacher who like really, really, you know, helps and support me in Australia and an English teacher was amazing out in Australia. And then to have that. But I had a great time at the grammar school. They like, they picked it up. They supported me. They got me extra time. They were brilliant. My brain skyrocketed.
>
> **What did you do next:** I wanted to go to university. I pushed it and I got there.

By the time that they have reached their A levels, most students have a sense of what they are good at and enjoy. However, that does not mean that they know what's next and how to get there if they choose university. Focussing on what they enjoy and what they can see themselves doing for the next three or four years is vital; it is a long time to do something that they don't like!

Metacognition is important to consider too. Talk to your students about how they learn, what study strategies they find useful and their preferred type of assessments. Different subjects work differently and within subjects, different universities have different ways of delivering courses or assessing their students. This is where university prospectuses are important for your students; they can really get insight about the subjects they enjoy, what they might like to study, where and, linked to that, the type of course they'd like to pursue.

It is also important to talk to your students about any access arrangements or specific ways of working they have found useful in school. Different universities or HE providers have different evidence requirements for arrangements such as extra time or scribes, so it is vital that they talk to each university and find out what will be needed to ensure that they have what they need. Students can apply for 'Disabled Students' Allowance' to help with the costs associated with having a specific learning difficulty. This usually requires a formal assessment from an appropriately qualified practitioner. The key thing is talking about the challenges of dyslexia and making sure your students know that they can apply for disability associated finances. Dyslexia does have some really strong, positive elements but also, it is vital to acknowledge that dyslexia can make HE study harder. Reading can be challenging. Writing can be excruciating. Students need to know that they are entitled to adjustments, and we need to help them access them.

Working and Part-time Study

Your students may not take up full-time study. Often we don't know the very private and personal battles that other people are experiencing at home; sadly this is the same for young people in schools. Some young people's capacity to pursue 'traditional' pathways into higher education may be limited by challenges in their personal lives. Even if seemingly feasible on paper, those students may need to stay near home or to take on a smaller studyload than their peers. Showing those students alternative ways to 'do' university/a degree whilst meeting their other commitments or responsibilities is vital.

Remote or blended learning can be a game-changer. It allows students to tackle courses in smaller chunks but still pursue their aims. Part-time study can be very helpful for individuals with dyslexia; they set their own pace of study and manage their workload as they need to. Taking on less and doing it over a longer time period can be really helpful, for example where students need to work alongside their studies or need more time to make sense of their learning. Students can also get student loans if their courses have a 'load' of 25 percent or more but it is important to contact their institution to clarify.

Sometimes, seeing the ten year plan can be intimidating and chunking it into bitesize pieces can seem foreboding. However, it is doable.

Overall, when considering university and higher education, students need to know that there is flexibility in how to get there. They don't have to do everything full-time and complete A Levels. They may want to take a flexible degree or they may want to do it part-time alongside something else. Talking to your students about the whole picture of what they see for themselves in those first few years after school can help them work out their own ten year plan.

Vocational

I wholly believe that there is no one 'vocational pathway'. There are many different routes through further education and onto higher education or work, which could be classified as vocational. I tend to think of pathways that do need training and are skills as 'vocational'. That is my personal view but it's not completely removed from the options out there. Talking Futures (Undated) lists options for students interested in pursuing a vocational route once they have left school. Importantly they also highlight the challenges that young people have in making informed decisions around career pathways at 14, 16 and 18 years old. They have found that young people don't know potential pathways forward and often need to have support from parents, teachers and other professionals to help them decide what to do in the next stage of their education.

Apprenticeships

Apprenticeships are where young people have a job that also provides training in a particular trade or skillset. The job that young people take at this stage is often a paid role, where their work impacts meaningfully on clients/customers. Alongside their role, young people may attend college or be supported in learning the requisite skills for their trade. Apprenticeships are available at all levels, with a large proportion of young people starting at level 2 (Higher GCSE pass equivalent) or 3 (A level equivalent). How they are advertised and applied for varies locally but there are national databases of vacancies within each of the home nations.

Apprenticeships are covered by exam and coursework regulations (British Dyslexia Association, Undated), and also the Special Educational Needs Code of Practice (DfE and DfH, 2015). This means that any support young people had in their school or college, before starting the apprenticeship should remain in place as students continue their training. Funding is available to training providers, and many free or low-cost resources exist to help people understand what dyslexia is and how it affects people in the workplace.

Lots of people take vocational routes who are not necessarily interested in going through university; success looks very different for different people. The creativity and excellent problem-solving skills that many people with dyslexia have can mean that they are really well suited to working in hands-on, practical settings where problems are tangible and real-world, in real-time.

T Levels and other Qualifications

T-levels were set up by the government as a way for students to pursue a vocational pathway but not cut off the possibility of attending university. They last for two years and are equivalent to three A levels. They were started officially in September 2020 which means that, at the time of writing, two cohorts have completed them. A fundamental difference between T Levels and apprenticeships is that they are only offered at level 3, and students who take a place on them must have higher passes in GCSE maths and English, or achieve this by the end of their course. Their core elements include gaining technical skills, and applying those general skills in industrial placements, whilst developing specific skills for the chosen occupation. T Levels are graded and have UCAS points values. Many universities accept T Levels as entry qualifications so students can both gain practical skills, and also progress onto higher education should they choose to. As above, students on these courses are covered by JCQ Access Arrangements regulations and the Special Educational Needs and Disability Code of Practice (DfE and DfH, 2015).

The Scenic Route

In this life, trajectories and journeys do not look the same for everyone for a myriad of reasons. Given the variety of pathways that people take after their compulsory schooling is complete, and the differing reasons that they have for that, I think the best way to see them in action is to share people's own journeys. My own journey was linear: through school, onto 6th form, a gap year with work experience and then university. So I am not best placed to share that element of my story here. My quirky pathway really only began after university when I started working out what really made me tick. So here are two other people's stories.

These stories were shared as part of the research for this book by amazing people, both of whom I've known in various contexts for a while. I've met Hannah in person on a few occasions and I've nothing but respect for her. I've not yet met Malcolm in person at the time of writing, which is a shame, as we live nearby. However, we have been in touch on social media for a good few years. Their stories have been edited here because they are based on email exchanges and discussions. The names here are not the individuals' real names to protect their privacy and confidentiality, and the wording may not be theirs in places, but the stories are!

Malcolm

In his own words: At school, I wanted to be a scientist or an engineer. But I never was – and never could have been – for the simple reason that I was in the lowest set for everything and left without a single exam result. Despite this, at age 14, I could dismantle a broken TV set and build a radio transmitter from the parts, and I had a self-taught understanding of electromagnetic propagation and Einstein's relativity theories. So why couldn't I keep up in class and pass my exams? What was happening to me at school was so different to what was going on in my head. Over the years this created a profound cognitive dissonance. It was a terrible time – and I turned to drugs and alcohol and slid into poor mental health. At the age of 21, I had an acute psychotic breakdown. Although this was harsh, it was a blessing in disguise – an opportunity to reboot my life. So I built my own yacht. Sailed four times across the Atlantic. Ran a successful charter business in the Caribbean and became an amateur pilot. Maybe I wasn't so stupid? At age 39, I became a mature student. I got very good marks, but writing an essay was a massive effort – and some things that should have been easy were almost impossible. But, thanks to an excellent tutor, I was diagnosed with dyslexia and language processing disorder. I wasn't alone. I discovered that, even now, 80 percent of dyslexia goes undiagnosed. So began my personal EDI journey based on a need to prevent others from having similar hard starts in life. We are on the same mission really, so I would like to help if I can!

Malcolm now works near to a leading university and his work is pioneering within the assistive/educational technology space. He has had a varied journey both professionally and academically but university was not the pathway that called him. He is highly skilled and a very sought after individual whose knowledge is valued by others. His dyslexia framed his pathway and nudged him along ways that might not have been on the radar of other people. Journeys like Malcolm's are so important to share with our students, who may feel that that they are failures, or who may not see avenues for their skills. Malcolm changed pathways and fields a few times as he progressed through education and into his professional life. He has accomplished (and continues to accomplish) amazing things!

Literacy Learning Journeys

Hannah

This is a summary that I've written based on what Hannah shared with me in a chat we had during summer 2023.

> Hannah is dyslexic and has various other disabilities that do make things very challenging for her. She has recently graduated and is now starting off her career in an exciting role working to diversify the student body of a small university in the South of England. She is in her late 30s and although she did start university when she was 18, she found that it was not the right thing for her in that moment. Hannah subsequently decided not to pursue higher education at that point in her life.
>
> Hannah worked very hard when she was in school and was determined to do well, giving over her lunchtimes to study and spending time after school, working hard across the board, but focussing particularly on her English. She always felt that she had challenges in her working memory. She worked hard to try and compensate for those challenges but Hannah was not supported at school for the difficulties she had. Hannah's dyslexia was initially identified when she started studying just after she had completed her A Levels. She found that reading aloud was very challenging for her and her tutors supported her to be fully and formally assessed for dyslexia. Hannah did find the process helpful and understood herself better after being diagnosed. However, as she was dealing with the implications of dyslexia and working to pay for studies, alongside full-time university study, Hannah decided that she needed to take some time away from studying so that other aspects of her life could flourish. She left university and started to work with young people in an Early Years setting.
>
> Hannah pursued this career and was highly successful, developing her own knowledge and supporting young people in the setting, as well as having her own family in the meantime. Hannah's journey was largely vocational, and she was highly qualified as an early years practitioner but she decided that, for her, it was important to gain formal academic recognition of the vocational experience and qualifications that she had from her work setting. So in her late 30s with a successful career already, Hannah decided to go back to university. Whilst doing this, she supported her children whose needs are

complex, alongside working. Hannah's journey at university was also varied and she did several projects related to supporting students with special needs at her university. Her role led her to being offered work within her university and her journey is just on the up!

Neither Hannah nor Malcolm has followed a run-of-the-mill journey as they have left school and entered the world of work, but they are both extremely successful and happy in what they do. There are other things that they both want to achieve but those goals relate to both their dyslexia and are informed by the diverse ways that they have engaged with education at various times. And crucially, their goals are informed by the ways that they chose *not* to engage with formal education at points across their careers so far.

School and Beyond: Dyslexic Legacies

There are many conclusions that could be drawn at this point in the book; we are near the end and hopefully you've found what you've read so far useful. The previous chapters have focussed on what dyslexia looks like and how we, as educators, can make little changes in delivery of the curriculum to support young people with dyslexia. This chapter has been about the journeys that young people may follow as they leave school. The following sections largely summarise the thought processes that we've introduced in this chapter and help you know the kinds of questions to ask your students as you support them in making choices about where to go next!

Things to Consider at Work

Support students to follow pathways that bring them joy. There are a large number of post-16 and post-18 pathways that young people can pursue and not one of those is the 'correct' way. People spend a long time at work and doing something that they don't enjoy can negatively impact wellbeing. It's important to remind young people that there are always 'boring' bits to a job but in an ideal world, the boring bits are countered by enjoyable and interesting elements. Dyslexia will always be part of young people's profiles, but there are workarounds, which hopefully they found in school and that they can now apply in their work context.

Dyslexic Strengths

Dyslexic individuals are creative and have many exciting strengths that can be vital in a workplace. The ability to step back and look at problems from a different perspective, the capacity to visualise things in different ways from others and the ability to explain things from a different point of view are invaluable in many different professions. Kate Griggs (2018) explains those strengths and gives great insight into the different career pathways that dyslexic people may take. Those careers wholly capitalise on the different abilities that dyslexic people have!

Challenges, Workarounds and the Law

Although there are many strengths associated with dyslexia, I think we need to acknowledge the challenges that arise for people who have it. Reading, remembering, writing and making sense of information can all be very difficult. There are workarounds which can transform someone's work life and enable them to do their job well. Employer-awareness is often the most important thing; in researching this book, a recurring theme was that awareness and understanding whether from teachers or managers makes a huge difference on the ground. That awareness meant that individuals could do their job, or access the curriculum properly and flourish wherever they were.

Dyslexia is a protected characteristic under the law and so employers must make reasonable adjustments to support their employees in the same way schools do. This may be through programmes such as 'Access to Work' which covers the costs of equipment and support for people who need it, and/or through ongoing training. There are many cost-effective resources which can help employers better understand their obligations and how to support employees!

Key Takeaways

- Different people's pathways through school and beyond will vary but the key thing is that they feel supported in what they do.
- Dyslexia may mean that people struggle with some elements of literacy but they may love other aspects of it. It is vital not to make assumptions about what people may want to do, or what they enjoy.
- Not everyone will want to go to university. There are many other pathways to choose from!

Further Reading

Success

- This chapter is focussed on understanding different journeys post-16 and post-18, depending on when young people choose to leave school and go their own way. Drivers for success vary for different individuals but so often it seems like 'success' is narrow and contingent on university and traditional career pathways.

- A key takeaway from this book is that we need to support young people to see success in their own way. If they don't want to go to university, we need to support them in that, and help them explore other pathways and options. If they choose university, we need to help our students make the best choices along those lines too.
- Success looks different for all our students, and we need to help them feel that in their bones!

Pathways

There are many different pathways through school and they won't necessarily all be suitable for everyone.

- For more information on different routes your students might want to explore after school, explore Talking Futures: https://www.talkingfutures.org.uk/pathways-at-16/#:~:text=There%20are%20several%20pathways%20for,learning%20whilst%20working%20or%20volunteering.
- The National Careers Service : https://nationalcareers.service.gov.uk/careers-advice/career-choices-at-16.
- Prospects : https://www.prospects.ac.uk/further-education/post-16-career-choices.
- Disabled students' allowance for students in England: https://www.gov.uk/disabled-students-allowance-dsa/eligibility.
- Disabled students' allowance in Scotland: https://www.saas.gov.uk/guides/dsa/dsa-allowances.
- Disabled students' allowance in Wales: https://www.studentfinancewales.co.uk/undergraduate-finance/full-time/welsh-student/what-s-available/disabled-students-allowance/.
- Disabled students' allowance in Northern Ireland: https://www.studentfinanceni.co.uk/types-of-finance/postgraduate/northern-ireland-student/extra-help/disabled-students-allowance/what-is-it/.
- There is information for training providers on funding to support young people with learning difficulties and disabilities: https://assets.publishing.service.gov.uk/government/uploads/system/uploads/attachment_data/file/1112154/Learning_support_funding_for_apprentices_with_learning_difficulties_and_disabilities.pdf.

References and Further Reading

Alexander-Passe, N. (2023) *Dyslexia, Neurodiversity, and Crime: Investigating the 'School to Prison Pipeline'*. Lewes, DE: DIO Press Inc.

Antonelli, L. et al. (2014) 'Drama, performance ethnography, and self-esteem: Listening to youngsters with dyslexia and their parents'. *SAGE Open*, 4(2), p. 215824401453469. https://doi.org/10.1177/2158244014534696.

British Dyslexia Association (Undated) 'Further education/apprenticeships, British Dyslexia association'. Available at: https://www.bdadyslexia.org.uk/advice/adults/in-education/further-education-apprenticeships (Accessed: 27 September 2023).

Department for Education (DfE) (2020) *16 to 18 destination measures (revised) Guidance and technical note for 2019 performance tables*. Available at: https://assets.publishing.service.gov.uk/government/uploads/system/uploads/attachment_data/file/859557/Destination_guidance_KS4_and_1618_2019.pdf.

Department for Education (DfE) and Department for Health (DfH) (2015) *Special Educational Needs and Disability Code of Practice: 0 to 25 Years*. London: DfE and DfH. Available at: https://assets.publishing.service.gov.uk/government/uploads/system/uploads/attachment_data/file/398815/SEND_Code_of_Practice_January_2015.pdf (Accessed: 5 August 2021).

Griggs, K. (2018) 'The value of Dyslexia'. Available at: https://www.madebydyslexia.org/assets/downloads/EY-the-value-of-dyslexia.pdf (Accessed: 23 February 2023).

Higginbotham, D. (2022) 'Post-16 career choices | Prospects.ac.uk, prospects'. Available at: https://www.prospects.ac.uk/further-education/post-16-career-choices (Accessed: 19 September 2023).

HMSO (2010) *Equality Act 2010*. Statute Law Database. Available at: https://www.legislation.gov.uk/ukpga/2010/15/contents (Accessed: 15 February 2022).

Kannangara, C. et al. (2018) 'Not all those who wander are lost: Examining the character strengths of Dyslexia'. *Global Journal of Intellectual & Developmental Disabilities*, 4(5). https://doi.org/10.19080/GJIDD.2018.04.555648.

Nalavany, B.A., Carawan, L.W. and Brown, L.J. (2011) 'Considering the role of traditional and specialist schools: Do school experiences impact the emotional well-being and self-esteem of adults with dyslexia?' *British Journal of Special Education*, 38(4), pp. 191–200. https://doi.org/10.1111/j.1467-8578.2011.00523.x.

O'Brien, T. and Guiney, D. (2021) 'Wellbeing: How we make sense of it and what this means for teachers'. *Support for Learning*, 36(3), pp. 342–355. https://doi.org/10.1111/1467-9604.12366.

Talking Futures (Undated) 'Pathways from 16+'. *Talking Futures*. Available at: https://www.talkingfutures.org.uk/pathways-at-16/ (Accessed: 27 September 2023).

9
Concluding Thoughts and Further Reading

Introduction

This chapter is where the different themes and ideas in this book are brought together. We have already seen that dyslexia can impact differently across the Key Stages, as the demands of the curriculum evolve. The main players in supporting children and young people with dyslexia are all important, with their different roles and perspectives being vital in making sure children are best supported to flourish as they progress through school. There are many ways that members of the stakeholder triad (in Chapter 7) can work to support children depending on their capacity, role and specific interests in dyslexia. In this chapter, we look at those different avenues but first, we look at the philosophical frameworks that need to underpin and inform how those stakeholders work together. I share some of my personal experience too; sometimes it is better to share from my own lived experience rather than trying to shoehorn other people's comments and stories into something specific as core ethics. My core ethics are wholly and completely intertwined with the professional journey that has brought me to where I am today. So I am sharing those experiences with you and hopefully it'll help you work through your own journey.

❓ Reflection Point: Your Motivation, Role and Capacity

With the best will in the world, no one person can know everything, be everything to everyone and still have time to enjoy a broad social life! Teachers are some of the most hard-working professionals, and long working hours, particularly at term time, are often part-and-parcel of the job. Parents of young people with SEND also have a demanding role in supporting their children, and that role takes up a lot of time and emotional labour. We are coming towards the end of the book and it seems a good time to think about what's next for you in your position with supporting young people with dyslexia. However, before jumping into the next thing to do, take a moment to think about the following:

- Why have you read this book and what has it inspired in you? What makes you want to do more about supporting young people with dyslexia?
- At the moment, what is your role in working with dyslexic children? What do you hope to do or achieve looking forwards? How do you see your role developing in the near and further future? What can you do to start to make those changes?
- If you have some ideas of what you might be able to do to develop your role, what are you able to commit to? Do you have spare time or is there something you can give up to make space in your schedule so that you can take the steps necessary in developing your role? Here it is so important to be aware of your limits and other commitments; don't take on too much!

Considering those elements of your own context is really important so that you don't overcommit, and potentially find yourself working on projects or studying for courses that are not right for you at the present time. That is not to say that it will never be the right pathway forward for you, but considering the here and now whilst planning the future is really important.

An Ethical and Philosophical Perspective

Although linked to higher education, Hamilton and Petty (2023: 1) advocate for a 'compassionate curriculum' to be implemented where 'interventions designed to create contexts in which neurodivergent people can thrive are needed'. This chimes with teaching expectations for those starting out within an English context. 'Adaptive teaching', where needs are pre-empted and addressed as part of overall provision forms part of early career teacher frameworks (Pope et al., 2021) links to a 'universal design for learning' paradigm, which is explained in the context of use of technology by Reid, Strnadová and Cumming (2013). I think that to implement inclusive, adaptive strategies in the classroom, when working with young people, understanding their perspective is vital. For me, this chimes wholly and entirely with Universal Design for Learning; as professionals working with young people, we need to make an active choice (kindness) to understand children's journeys and experiences (empathy), but this does not come instantly and can mean that we need to work alongside them for a period of time to gain that understanding properly. I think that you will not make too many awful mistakes if you do hold kindness, empathy and time as part of your 'core values' when you work with young people in general!

Kindness

I think kindness is an underrated and under-implemented quality in this life. Sometimes it can seem like kind people get walked all over but I disagree; sometimes kindness can mean standing up for something or someone tooth and nail, in spite of everything against you seeming to make it impossible to do so. Sometimes kindness can lead to confrontation, but through those conflicts, crunch points or challenging times, if you are working to support someone, your kindness will be strong and unwavering. Kindness is by no means a non-committal, flaky quality that just flaps in the wind. It can be stoic and vital in people's journeys.

Often, I am asked for advice on what people need, or who people should talk to. I don't always feel that I know exactly what to say, or who to refer people to, or the best course of action. However, after I've listened to people talk through their situation, they have thanked me for my kindness.

I don't always feel like I have been particularly kind but on reflection, and as I write now, sometimes actively listening and giving people space to talk is kind. Antonelli *et al.* (2014) allude to just that in their paper; listening to people can be one of the most important things on their journey.

What kindness looks like in your own setting, and from your perspective will differ from others, but you know what you would appreciate, so in the first instance I would say, give that to other people as you work with them. It does reap rewards; sometimes it can even bring a little tear to the eye!

Empathy

Empathy does not come out of nowhere. To feel empathy with someone, I think it is really important to listen to them, watch their journey and take on anything they tell you about it. Empathy does not come from a place of presumption and assumption but rather from a place of listening and kindness. With young people (and potentially colleagues) who are dyslexic, each experience and manifestation is different – we have already seen this in the book – so making assumptions about what they want/need to have in place to help them may be counterproductive. Listen, spend time and take on how others experience their dyslexia so you can start to empathise with their position and work out with them how to make it better.

Time

Everything in this life takes time and it seems to be the *most* finite of resources. It is also one of the most important things to take and use to build relationships and show yourself kindness. Sometimes we can get caught up in the day to day whirlwind of life and feel like there is no time to do things that might actually save us time in the long run. Sometimes it can be really useful to step back, and reflect on what time you can spend, so that you can then take time to build kindness and empathy, as you interact with young people, and into the curriculum as *you* deliver it! That time will pay dividends as you start to develop ways to support children and their families; you will have been kind to yourself too!

Name: Dr Helen Ross

Role: SEND Consultant, Researcher and Specific Learning Difficulties expert

What prompted a change? I found myself having less and less time with my family when I was working in a full-time SENDCO job. There were some lovely people in the school and there were elements of the job that I loved but I found that I wasn't using my PhD in the role and pressures of the role were outweighing the benefits.

How was I kind? This may seem to be entirely counter-intuitive to the process of kindness, because I did potentially cause myself a lot of stress as I worked through my pathways forwards. After a really tricky time and some time away in Berlin on holiday with Mr Dr Ross, I decided to hand in my notice.

How did I create empathy for myself? Anyone who knows me personally would probably say that I do not show myself the grace or empathy that I would show other people who were in a place where they needed to make some changes to their life, be it in a professional or a personal capacity. I was at a point where I did need to stop and take stock of what I was aiming for work-wise and how that might impact on me, and those around me, personally. I had talked through different pathways forward with Mr Dr Ross and we had a bit of a plan. Through talking to Mr Dr Ross, I realised what I would say to someone else in the position that I was in: go easy on yourself and move on.

So I did.

I left my job and started to look for the next thing. Then I found it and started to work towards where I am now work-wise.

What time did I take? I took time to step back and work through what I was feeling with a trusted member of my family; in my case it was my husband but different people have different journeys and may find that exploring their current situation will not always be with someone in their circle. We happened to have a holiday booked at a time that fitted just perfectly with when I needed to make changes, so we used that time and the time on coming home to just revisit my choices from time to time. Between that Easter holiday in Berlin and the following summer, I concocted a plan to train as a dyslexia/specific learning difficulties assessor and to work independently doing that alongside research. It was not easy but it was the right decision for me.

What am I doing now to keep it up? Taking time and creating empathy for myself does not always come easily. During the process of writing this book, I was diagnosed with ADHD, which helped me to understand why I have the thought processes that I do and why I really do overpack my schedule. I am starting to take more time to work out if I want to do things, how I want to do them or if I just want to say no. I don't get it right all the time and Mr Dr Ross and a few other very close friends, who are valued very much, do tell me when I'm being a plonker to myself or doing too much. So to keep myself in a good place, as much as I can, I have a really solid group of friends that I can turn to, and who are not 'yes people'. I need people to call me out when needed but who do so from a place of support and to edify not criticise.

❓ Reflection Point: Showing Kindness, Empathy and Time towards Yourself

You cannot be everything to everyone. That is a fact and sometimes we do not do the things for ourselves that we suggest to others. Showing kindness to ourselves, taking a step back and making sure we empathise with our own position (both struggles and good points!) takes time. Sometimes we forget to do that. It is so important to make sure we look after our own wellbeing so that we can then support others around us. Think on the following and make notes if it helps:

- When was the last time that you did something just for you, that didn't relate to work, or supporting your family or doing someone else a favour? Just for you, no one else. If you can't think of it, think of something that you can do, just for you!
- When was the last time you gave yourself grace for something that you would show others, but don't often show yourself? You

> might have made a mistake, or upset someone, forgotten something? When did you forgive yourself for something like that, as you would a friend or colleague?
>
> These are all easy to say, I realise that, and I'm as guilty as anyone else of *not* being kind to myself, but I do my best, and hopefully I'm getting better!

Educator Support

There is a lot of training and information available, both online and in the real world, for people who have an interest in working with children with dyslexia. Some of it is very helpful and practical while other trainings may not be so pragmatic. Types and length of course vary, as do the kinds of resources available, according to the level of training you want and how (if at all) you hope for it to be accredited. These different issues are addressed here, with some links to further reading given. It is important to say that I have not done all these courses but I have researched their content. You may find them useful or you may not but if you want to do them, I would say that it is vital that you contact the providers before signing up formally.

What is Needed When Working with Dyslexic Children?

When working with dyslexic children, it is important that professionals have awareness of the challenges of dyslexia. You will need to know what it is; trying to work to support children with dyslexia without knowing what it is would be very challenging. There are many different ways that dyslexia can show up in the classroom so you will need to have awareness of those manifestations and then what to do about them. There are various checklists that can be applied when you are looking to identify dyslexia, with some of them linking to identifiable targets and associated support strategies. You may find that you are working with one or more dyslexic learners and want practical insight into strategies to help them; multi-sensory resources are vital here, and sometimes approaches other than phonics-based ones are useful. For example morphological strategies can reap rewards. Ways to help them record learning differently can be helpful and gaining insight into assistive technology is helpful in this process. If you want to be able to formally identify and assess people to see if they may have dyslexia, there are also formally accredited pathways to do so, whether that is via Specialist Assessor routes or an Educational Psychology pathway. No one person is likely to fulfil these different roles but they are all equally important and can be better carried out with additional training. Some roles also mandate specialist and accredited training. There are some links to different pathways, practice resources and professional development resources below.

Short Courses, Informal CPD, and Other Resources

There is a huge range of short courses relating to dyslexia that can be accessed online. I will give an overview of different courses. They are ordered in the sequence that they showed when I ran a search online using the key words 'face to face dyslexia training'. Not all the results were face to face courses so I have listed the different types of courses and given an overview of their providers. This list is by no means exhaustive, but hopefully it will give you somewhere to start.

- PATOSS runs a wide variety of courses that are accessible for both members and non-members. Some courses are accredited formally and offer CPD hours while others are for information. There are some that are a couple of hours long, and others that are a more substantive course, leading to a level 1, 2, or 3 certificate. Information about their different courses, remote, blending and in-person, is here: https://www.patoss-dyslexia.org/all-events.
- Positive Dyslexia is run by Katrina Cochrane, who was formerly part of the Senior Management Team at the BDA. The company offers courses for Needs Assessors in the workplace, as well as level 3 and 4 training. They also run bespoke training for organisations and run conferences regularly. Have a look here for more information. https://www.positivedyslexia.co.uk/ocn-accredited-training/accredited-training/
- Communicate-ed runs short courses for educators on various topics. Their dyslexia course is a two hour short course for those supporting

Concluding Thoughts and Further Reading

dyslexic students. You can look at the details of the course here: https://www.communicate-ed.org.uk/courses/supporting-students-with-dyslexia.

- For different approaches to literacy, teaching strategies such as morphology or etymology can be useful. There are various people who have expertise in these approaches so internet searches are likely to be fruitful. Individuals such as Louise Selby offer bespoke training in person or pre-recorded, depending on what you need. Her website is here: https://louiseselbydyslexia.com/.
- Short courses exist online which offer more than an INSET session but give more flexibility than a formal certificate. For example, Yale University offers this course (although the title is not necessarily helpful, there are some useful elements): https://www.coursera.org/learn/dyslexia.
- Microsoft runs courses in collaboration with Made by Dyslexia and many universities also offer MOOCs, which can sometimes be counted towards CPD hours.

Formalised Learning and Accredited Pathways

There are various routes that can be taken to gain qualifications to assess for and identify dyslexia. The principle routes in the UK are via Educational Psychologist training or Specialist Assessor training. There is some information about this here. These links were accessed in June 2024, but in case they have been altered since I accessed them, I have included the names of the relevant organisations here too.

- **Educational Psychologists** take a professional doctorate over three years. The doctorate can be funded by the individual who is taking up the doctoral study. However, there is also a funded route that lasts for six years, with three years as a doctoral student, followed by three years working for a local authority or another setting that undertakes statutory work for a Local Authority. There is a limited number of places for this pathway annually and it is very competitive. Further information on training to become an Educational Psychologist is available from the Association of Educational Psychologists. They provide information on training in England, Scotland, Wales and Northern Ireland. The link to how to train is here: https://www.aep.org.uk/interested-career-educational-psychology.
- There are several routes to becoming a **Specialist Assessor or Teacher**. There are different levels of accreditation: to be a specialist teacher you can complete a 'level 5' course but to formally assess for dyslexia, a 'level 7' (Masters level) is necessary. Some of these are university based, others are run by accredited providers online and other pathways offer blended learning. I have included courses on offer from various providers as they are delivered differently and may suit people depending on their context.

Level 5 Courses
There are various providers that run courses for those interested in formalising their knowledge and professional development around supporting children with literacy difficulties. A lot of the courses are online and searching online will bring up useful links. If completing an accredited course is a priority for you, a key thing to look for is that any course you take would qualify your for membership of one of the main professional bodies for those working with dyslexic students: the British Dyslexia Association, the Dyslexia Guild, or PATOSS.

- Helen Arkell runs two different level 5 courses for teaching learners with dyslexia/specific learning difficulties. One is aimed at those working in Key Stages 1 and 2, while the other is aimed at those who support young people in Key Stages 2 and 3. You can find more information here: https://helenarkell.org.uk/level-5-and-level-7/.
- The Learning Support Centre runs a level 5 course for teaching learners with dyslexia and specific learning difficulties. This qualifies people to join PATOSS, the Dyslexia Guild, the BDA and ADSHE (Association of Dyslexia Specialists in Higher Education). Further information is here: https://learningsupportcentre.com/level-5-diploma/.
- Dyslexia Matters is run by two dyslexia specialists who have a wide range of experience in supporting learners. Their courses have the advantage of being approved for Enhanced Learning Credits Administration Services (ELCAS) funding, so those who are applying from within the Ministry of Defence may qualify for funding to help cover the costs of the course. More information is here: https://www.dyslexiamatters.co.uk/level-5-premium-specialist-teacher-programme/.

Level 7 Courses

Level 7 courses lead to practitioners being able to apply for an Assessment Practising Certificate (APC), which is overseen by the Specific Learning Difficulties Assessment Standards Committee. Details of how APCs work are given on the SASC website: https://www.sasc.org.uk/assessment-practising-certificate/. Awarding organisations that can grant APCS are the British Dyslexia Association, the Dyslexia Guild and PATOSS (the Professional Association of Teachers of Students with Specific Learning Difficulties). Each of these organisations has its own website and membership process but they all must meet SASC criteria. It is not obligatory to maintain an APC, but it is formal recognition of CPD and also means that assessments can be used to apply for Disabled Students' Allowance.

- An overview of routes to becoming a dyslexia specialist with the BDA is here: https://cdn.bdadyslexia.org.uk/uploads/documents/Flow-chart-for-accreditation-1.pdf?v=1691042510.
- There is a list of courses approved by the British Dyslexia Association, which leads to accreditation as a specialist assessor. The list may vary as different institutions apply for accreditation but it is available here: https://www.bdadyslexia.org.uk/services/accreditation/specialist-teacher

-accreditation/approved-teacher-status-ats-approved-practitioner-status-aps.
- Other providers such as Helen Arkell also run level 5 and 7 courses.
- Qualifications leading to membership of PATOSS are available here: https://www.patoss-dyslexia.org/qualifications-leading-to-membership. Again, they must be formally accredited and meet SASC criteria.
- Dyslexia Action offers a professional qualification for becoming an assessor in collaboration with Real Training. There is information here: https://dyslexiaaction.org.uk/postgraduate-level-qualifications-spld/.
- Dyslexia Matters offers an online course and details are available here: https://www.dyslexiamatters.co.uk/wp-content/uploads/2020/06/Outline-of-course-Level-7.pdf.
- The Dyslexia Guild's course links to Dyslexia Action but individuals who have an APC with other providers are able to apply with the Dyslexia Guild upon renewal of their certificate.

Family Support

A family whose child I assessed recently described the role of being the parent of a child with special educational needs/disability as a full-time job. This is not the first time I have heard that and it does seem that sometimes, engaging with SEND systems can be somewhat daunting for families, meaning that resources are de facto gatekept by schools even if it has not been an active decision or process to withhold certain interventions from young people. Here I give an overview of some of the things that families can find tricky and will offer links to some practical support strategies. I will also link to legal resources for those difficult times where relationships break down and support packages for student are not as expected or hoped for.

What Can Families Find Tricky?

There are many challenges that families can experience when working with systems that relate to special educational needs. Within the four home nations, the language linked to frameworks can be impenetrable, which is a barrier in itself for families whose children have dyslexia or other SEND. As children's provision becomes more specialist and where statutory provision may be implicated, those challenges can be amplified. This is even more so where formal legal proceedings may be entered; working with a legal team can be implicated here and processes can feel like they run away with themselves, leaving families behind.

Families can also struggle with the practical aspects of supporting their children. Often when I work with families, the first thing they ask is how they can help their children at home both with academic work and with their wider wellbeing. Families do not want to spend all their time arguing with their children about homework or battling over routines in the morning, so having some resources and suggestions to help along the way can be really useful.

Practical Support Resources

There are resources and strategies suggested at various points in this book, but here I have put a few key suggestions that may be useful as a starting point for you to support your teachers.

Literacy Support

- Although unexpected, there are some useful strategies on the UK government website. There are some suggestions for supporting children with reading here: https://www.gov.uk/government/publications/10-top-tips-to-encourage-children-to-read/10-top-tips-to-encourage-children-to-read.
- Twinkl has a wide range of resources for supporting families to engage with literacy and the wider curriculum. There are useful resources for literacy here, as well as help for parents in supporting their children's wellbeing. The suite of resources can be seen here, but using key words in the Twinkl website tends to lead to useful resources https://www.twinkl.co.uk/resources/free-resources-parents/for-parents-free-resources-parents/free-resources-for-parents-free-resources-parents. It is important to note that although there are free resources, some things are charged for.
- The National Literacy Trust also has a wide range of resources for families to support their children with literacy: https://literacytrust.org.uk/parents-and-families/.
- There are also lots of paid-for resources and websites that you may find useful. I think that it's really important to make sure you talk to your children's school before you subscribe to a service; anything you work on at home to support literacy development needs to work with in-school support so that children are not overloaded with input, or working on different elements of phonics in different settings. Working together to reinforce school at home and vice versa is important so that children get input 'little and often'.

Routine and Organisation Support

Challenges in organisation present in many neurodiversities. So these resources may be suitable for children with complex profiles, as well as children who do not appear to have learning challenges.

Concluding Thoughts and Further Reading

- Although this is aimed at supporting children with ADHD, because of the amount of cross-over with ADHD and dyslexia, the strategies and issues highlighted are relevant. The ADHD Centre offers various paid-for services and assessments but this set of suggestions is freely available and useful: https://www.adhdcentre.co.uk/adhd-advice-helping-child-overcome-organisation-problems/.
- Bradford City Council has compiled a document with a wide range of support strategies for children with SEND. Different strategies for various areas of the curriculum are offered and grouped together. This is a really comprehensive resource: https://bso.bradford.gov.uk/userfiles/file/Behaviour%20Support%20Service/SEBD%20Team/SENCo%20Induction%20Resources/2%20Strategies%20for%20Supporting%20Pupils%20with%20SEN%20PDF(1).pdf.
- There are some time management and organisation suggestions on the NHS website, which are helpful. They are aimed at helping children and young people. You can look at them here: https://cambspborochildrenshealth.nhs.uk/child-development-and-growing-up/time-management-and-organisation-skills/.

Legal Input

There are various levels of legal information that I think families need access to when they are engaging with schools and provision for their children.

Some background legal knowledge can be very useful so that parents know what is expected of them in various situations. It can also be useful for families to deepen their understanding of systems if they are working with statutory provision for their children. Frameworks, language and procedures can seem very rigid and unforgiving, so having some knowledge and training around those systems is often invaluable to make them accessible. Where things go awry, it can be necessary to seek formal legal advice. There are many 'levels' of advice that legal professionals can offer, depending on the need and resources available. There is some information here.

Overview and General Information

- Although this article is aimed at educators, it is helpful for getting an insight into the kind of language and structures involved in supporting children with SEND. Real Training provides training for teachers; they offer SENDCO qualifications, short courses and Masters level, accredited qualifications. They are a very well-known organisation and I have used their resources for Access Arrangements and found them very helpful! The article is here: https://realtraining.co.uk/2021/10/how-to-effectively-discuss-sen-with-parents.
- Local parent councils or support groups can offer a wealth of information about dyslexia support and wider SEND structures in a given area. Depending on where you are in the UK, you may refer to ALN or SEN but an internet search of your local area name and 'parent support for children with dyslexia' should offer some useful links.

Statutory Provision and Legal Structures

- SEN Action is a useful site for both training and for when relationships have broken down to the point where formal legal intervention is needed. This course sets up parents to be advocates for themselves and even aims to equip parents as far as the Tribunal process. Details are here: https://senaction.co.uk/parent-sen-advocacy-training-programme/.
- Local area parent support groups are also a useful source for information around statutory provision. As noted above, have an online search of your local area and statutory provision for children with learning needs.

You may find in person groups as well as training. Having that solidarity of knowing people, in real life, who have similar experiences as you is vital.

Legal Advice for Formal Proceedings

- Although this course is aimed at legal professionals and is relatively expensive, you may find it helpful if you are trying to avoid engaging a legal professional. MBL Seminars offer training to professionals, so it is always worth having that in mind, if you do look at this course. I would say that it's important to call them and talk to them before you decide to take any of their courses. The SEND Law course is here: https://www.mblseminars.com/courses/the-sen-regime-assisting-parents-and-children-learn-live.
- IPSEA offer legal training at various levels to different stakeholders in the SEND process. There are both online and in-person events detailed here: https://www.ipsea.org.uk/pages/category/training-for-parents-and-carers. I have included IPSEA here because they are a well-known, national organisation that offers a wide range of support and training, depending on what is needed at any point in time.

Young People Support

This book has focussed on those working with dyslexic children and young people, and this section of the final chapter does not divert from that focus. However, we also need to recognise that we are working with children and young people to support them towards independence, and to help empower them to advocate for themselves, navigate their own journey and progress on to move in the world as they need to, with the skills they need to tackle all aspects of life. So this section is aimed at those who work with older individuals, who are on the cusp of leaving formal education and who may need to be signposted to resources that will help them forge their own pathway was they move forwards.

Where Can Young People Struggle?

Accessing the written word can be a real struggle for young people and this impacts on tasks such as completing forms or accessing appropriate support at university. There may be challenges linked to learning new software and procedures associated with jobs or diary management. Curating a CV can be a challenge for even the most experienced individuals, so for young people who are starting out, it can be very daunting.

A sense of solidarity and community is important for anyone but more so for those who have spent their time in school feeling on the outside of academics, sports clubs and social scenes. Even so, leaving those sometimes-challenging walls of school can be very intimidating for children; they know how school works so being set 'free' into the world of work or higher education may be very intimidating. There are some resources detailed below that young people who you support may find helpful. As with everything in this book, the list is not exhaustive and there may be many other resources which are useful. I have also shared some resources made by young people for young people of different ages; sometimes hearing things from peers is vital and gives an insight that hearing older voices doesn't!

What Support Is There for Them, and By Them?

- Armelle McGeachie has the most amazing online presence and has a following on TikTok where she shares insights into what it is like being dyslexic and a girl, through work and as she navigates life. Her handle on TikTok is @girlswithdyslexia.
- Jo Rees offers insight into dyslexia and also has a large following on TikTok. She is a lively individual and offers the most wonderful advice for dyslexic people in all walks of life. Her handle is @dyslexiclifewithjorees.
- This thread on the 'Student Room' specifically addresses dyslexia at university https://www.thestudentroom.co.uk/showthread.php?t=1253625. There are also other threads that look at time management, organisation and challenges with social life, amongst other things. Looking at the site and exploring how to engage with the site will be useful for young people who are considering university. Knowing where to seek help is vital. There is also a sense of solidarity that can be found in online forums, as well as through TikTok and other social media.

- For students who may want to apply to university, there is a resource from the Complete University Guide for dyslexic students, covering funding, which university may be right and how you can meet your potential at university https://www.youtube.com/watch?v=CBEQxJK9Y6Q.
- Dyslexia Ireland has some useful resources and books signposted for students on their website: https://dyslexia.ie/info-hub/supports-for-young-people/useful-resources-for-young-people/.
- If young people are looking at entering the world of work, rather than going to university, they may find resources on managing their time helpful. Indeed.co.uk, which is a recruitment website, has articles to offer advice on navigating the work place for individuals. This article is useful for exploring time management: https://uk.indeed.com/career-advice/career-development/time-management-tips. More detail around time management is given below, as it is an area of substantial challenge for those with dyslexia.

Time Management

- Time management can be an area of substantial challenge for dyslexic people. Here are a few videos that offer some tips. They vary in length and style but offer some helpful strategies. The different styles are useful to address how different young people may engage:
    - This video is presented by Bernard Marr, who works in technology: https://www.youtube.com/watch?v=DgLcyBfLLvQ. His focus is on working smarter, and may suit young people who prefer shorter videos. This one is roughly four minutes long.
    - A five minute video on different strategies for teenagers is presented by Jen Mead using animations and graphics to demonstrate different ways to organise schedules. You can view it here: https://www.youtube.com/watch?v=CBEQxJK9Y6Q. Jen is a health educator and is passionate about supporting children with mental health difficulties, which do often impact on dyslexic individuals.

My Final Word

This book has been a labour of love for the most part, but I have found some of the chapters tricky to write because of the challenges I experienced in school and sometimes in my working life. As I've said in other chapters, a major motivator for me in all the work I do is to help empower young people with dyslexia (and other SEND) so that they can take on the world and be their best selves. This will look different for everyone at different stages in their education and is likely to change for those people as they grow up and find out more about themselves. For me, I think one of the most important things that we need to remember about education in general (whether children have SEND or otherwise) is that the 'outputs' and journeys onwards will look different for every individual. There is no one, correct pathway forwards. Our job as educators, parents and human beings alongside other human beings, is to listen to each other and help each other along the way, to be our best selves.

I hope this book has given you some useful thoughts and ideas around how you can work with dyslexic students in whatever role you occupy, so that they can flourish. That is what we are all aiming for, after all!

Key Takeaways

- Time is key for supporting young people with dyslexia. The stress on their verbal processing and working memory in the classroom setting can be overwhelming, so taking that pressure off can be transformational. It can help them to have enough capacity to engage better with learning and also in social settings! Young people's social time is as important as academic time, so anything we can do to help facilitate that is invaluable.
- Kindness and empathy need to underpin interactions and support strategies for young people. Individuals can usually perceive how others feel about them and their relationship, so if there is a rocky foundation for interactions, children and their families will know. Mutual kindness and respect leads to positive relationships, where meaningful dialogue, active listening and appropriate actions can be fostered.
- Relationships and empowerment are key: choice and independence are written into the DNA of the SEND Code of Practice (DfE and DfH, 2015). While structures and processes within the policy may not always operate as smoothly as hoped, the overarching principles within SEND policy documentation aim to support children/young people to be independent and to make informed choices. We need to make sure that how we act and the strategies we use do not ride roughshod over those ideals, even where systems may be lacking. Active and meaningful listening is vital to support this, and should be part of all our interactions as we work with young people.
- Each child/young person is different, as are those working with them. Different people will have different motivations for seeking further information/training around dyslexia and their capacity to engage with training will also vary. There is a diverse range of pathways that people can take and some of those are highlighted in this book.
- Key words such as 'dyslexia support', 'strategies', 'inclusion' and your local area name, or main town, can provide a wealth of information linked to support available near you. These resources may include parent/carer groups, which are often a goldmine of information and where the people who run them are usually passionate about supporting others. Working online and also building real-life connections is invaluable.

References and Bibliography

Antonelli, L. *et al.* (2014) 'Drama, performance ethnography, and self-esteem: Listening to youngsters with Dyslexia and their parents'. *SAGE Open*, 4(2), p. 215824401453469. https://doi.org/10.1177/2158244014534696.

Department for Education (DfE) and Department for Health (DfH) (2015) *Special Educational Needs and Disability Code of Practice: 0 to 25 Years*. London: DfE and DfH. Available at: https://assets.publishing.service.gov.uk/government/uploads/system/uploads/attachment_data/file/398815/SEND_Code_of_Practice_January_2015.pdf (Accessed: 5 August 2021).

Hamilton, L.G. and Petty, S. (2023) 'Compassionate pedagogy for neurodiversity in higher education: A conceptual analysis'. *Frontiers in Psychology*, 14, p. 1093290. https://doi.org/10.3389/fpsyg.2023.1093290.

Pope, R. *et al.* (2021) *Early Career Framework*. Department for Education and the Education Endowment Foundation. Available at: https://assets.publishing.service.gov.uk/media/60795936d3bf7f400b462d74/Early-Career_Framework_April_2021.pdf (Accessed: 8 May 2024).

Reid, G., Strnadová, I. and Cumming, T. (2013) 'Expanding horizons for students with dyslexia in the 21st century: universal design and mobile technology'. *Journal of Research in Special Educational Needs*, 13(3), pp. 175–181. Available at: https://doi.org/10.1111/1471-3802.12013.

Index

3D letters 45, 71, 95, 143

academic difficulties: literacy challenges 119–120; organisation 121; working memory and processing 120–121
academics 194; access courses 163, 164; apprenticeships and International Baccalaureate 163; approach 162; case study 163–164; disabled students' allowance 164–165; educators support 162; HE study harder 165; A levels 164; metacognition 164; pathways 162; post-16 pathways for young people 163; 'prospects' website 163; supporting *see* Supporting academics; working and part-time study 165; young people with dyslexia 162
access arrangements 192
access courses 163
Access to Work programmes 173
adaptive teaching 178
Additional Learning Needs Coordinators (ALNCOs) 140
ADHD 23: and dyslexia 191; and Tourette's 10
agency and power: funding 148; learning need dyslexia 148; measures 149; schools work 149; support frameworks for young people 148–149
ages of 3-4 children (speech and language): age 5 and upwards 34–35; basic speech sounds 34; knowledge 35–36; making sense of talking *35*; multisyllabic words 34; nursery rhymes, songs and stories 34; sounds 34; speech and language 33–34; words, knowledge of 33; work with complex sentences 34

ALN or SEN 192
anxiety 99, 115, 123, 134
apprenticeships: degree-apprenticeship 160; by exam and coursework regulations 167; and International Baccalaureate 163; proportion of young people, level 2 or 3 167; training, trade or skillset 167
Assessment Practising Certificate (APC) 187
Association of Dyslexia Specialists in Higher Education (ADSHE) 186
automaticity 89, 90
awareness, policy and practice *124;* dyslexia as disability and special education 124–128; expectations on organisations 123

babies and toddlers (from 0-3 years old): development, children's listening 33; face sounds 33; mimic lip movements 33
BDA *see* British Dyslexia Association (BDA)
boosting child and wellbeing 72
British Dyslexia Association (BDA) 17, 21–22, 24, 25, 48, 66, 150, 184, 186, 187; areas 21; conceptualisation, ICD 11 21; conceptualisation of literacy challenges 21; definition of dyslexia 21; educators to monitor progress 25; empowered dyslexic *22;* time of writing 25
British Psychological Society (BPS) 19, 28; assessing for dyslexia 19; dyslexia in UK *20;* spelling 20; underpinning cognitive processing challenges 19; website 28; word-level reading 20

Index

challenges: life after school 173; literacy 119; teachers and students 114; verbal processing 92
children: communication and language 53; education 2; finding rooms 114; literacy challenges 119; Lower Key Stage 2 *see* Lower Key Stage 2; vocabulary knowledge 34; volunteer 45
children's voice: case study 142; primary school 142, 143; secondary school 143; supporting 142; supporting students 144
classroom 197; dyslexia 123; Key Stage 2 92; UK 1
college 167
communicate-ed runs short courses 184–185
communication and language 53; frameworks, spoken word 40
communication skills 162
compulsory education 162
confidence boosting matters 66
CPD 187; dyslexia expert *188;* formal recognition 187; informal 184–185; and learning *185*
creativity and excellent problem-solving skills 167
curriculum: cross-curricular learning 107; demands 107; English context 57, 107; excellence 62, 110; frameworks (Wales) 107; impacts on timetable and subjects 110; Key Stage 1 51–52, 57; Key Stage 2 (7-11years old) 76, 86; National Curriculum for England 108–109; Northern Ireland 109; reliance 107; schools 110; Scotland 110; substantial differences 107; timetables 107, 108; timetable window 107; Wales 62–63; Welsh education system 109
curriculum for Wales 109; 130

delivery of the curriculum 172
Delphi definition 25
Department for Education 154
Department for Health 101
developmental coordination disorder 23
dialogue with students 124
dictation 59, 83, 126
disability associated finances 164–165
disabled students' allowance 187–188
DNA of the SEND Code of Practice 197
documented difficulties 112
dyscalculia 23
The Dyslexia Debate 15
Dyslexia Guild 186, 187
dyslexia support: CPD 184–185, *185;* ethical and philosophical perspective 178–182; family support *see* family support; formalised learning and accredited pathways 186–188; impacts, key stages 176; resources 197; short courses 184; stakeholder 176; students role 196; which way now? *177;* working with dyslexic children 183–184
dyslexic individuals 172
dyslexic-traits 51
dyslexic young people strengths 162

early years foundation status (EYFS): from EFYS to KS 1 *57;* experiences and expectations 58; formative progress tracking 56; learning goals 52, 57; programme 53; progression *53, 54;* and sequencing 60
education, health and care plans (EHCPs) 127, 138, 148
educational psychologists 186; training 186
educational psychology pathway 184
education authorities 140
educators' voice: case study 147–148; dyslexic children's support interventions 147; experience of young people 147; role of SENDCO 146; SEND systems 146; SEN framework 146; teaching assistants and pastoral support 146
EHCPs *see* education, health and care plans (EHCPs)
ELCAS *see* Enhanced Learning Credits Administration Services (ELCAS)
emotion effects of dyslexia 50
empathy 180, 182, 197
employer-awareness 173
England 18, 38, 56, 60, 62, 130, 140; cross-curricular sessions for students 108; Key Stages 3, 4 and 5, secondary school 108; National Curriculum for England 108; primary school experience 108–109
English education system 31

200

Index

English-language spelling conventions 71
Equality Act 2010 93, 124, 140, 153
ethical and philosophical perspectives: adaptive teaching 178; case study 181–182; compassionate curriculum 178; core values *179*; empathy 180; kindness 179–180; time 180; universal design for learning paradigm 178–179

family support: challenges 189; happy families *189*; homework or battling over routines 189; legal input 191–193; practical support strategies 189–191; role of parent 188; SEND systems 188; wellbeing 189
formalised learning and accredited pathways: educational psychologists 186; educational psychologist training 186; level 5 courses 186–187; level 7 courses 187–188; specialist assessor or teacher 186
freedom 161–162
free or low-cost resources 167
full-time study 165
funding, apprenticeship 167

GCSEs 109, 126, 128, 145, 159, 167; examinations 104; maths and English 167
general mark-making 83
government guidance 86
grammar and punctuation rules 85
grammatical constructions 83

handwriting 57; expectations 59; young people's 53–54
handwriting and composition: Lower Key Stage 2 83–84; Upper Key Stage 2 84–86
HE study 164, 165
higher education 178; settings 154
homophones and possessive apostrophes 83

ICT and assistive technology 129
identity-first language 12
International Classification of Diseases (ICD): and dyslexia *19;* individual's academic attainment 18; specific learning difficulties 18

International Dyslexia Association 28
interview 3, 40, 115, 142
IPSEA offer legal training 193

JCQ Access Arrangements regulations 129; 168
Job: apprenticeships 167; and training routes 160
Joint Council for qualifications 125

Key Stage 1: curriculum 51; literacy 62; music and drama 65; physical development 54; remembering verbal instructions 66–67; speech and language, age 5 and upwards 34–35; wider curriculum 60
Key Stage 2: case studies 87–88; curriculum 86; dyslexia 87; language and communication 33; lower *see* Lower Key Stage 2; upper *see* Upper Key Stage 2
kindness 179–180, 182, 197
knowledge: phonics 81; young people's 80

language and communication 53–54; early years and dyslexia 33–35
languages: and acquisition of knowledge 86; and communication *see* language and communication; development and literacy 36; frame dyslexia 18; skills 53; and terminology 12–13
learners support 76, 94
learning: aims 56; areas of development 56
learning goals: areas of development 52; EYFS 52
legacies, dyslexic 171–172, *171*
legal advice for legal proceedings 193
legal knowledge of family: advice for formal proceedings 193; background 192; frameworks, language and procedures 192; overview and general information 192; SEND law *191;* statutory provision and legal structures 192–193
letter naming 59
letters and sounds 41
A levels courses 163–165, 170
Local Area Parent Support Groups 192–193

201

Index

Local Authority/Academy Trust guidelines 127
Local Authority in England 127
local parent councils or support groups 192
long-term memory 92
lower and upper case letters 59
Lower Key Stage 2: handwriting and composition 83–84; reading comprehension 80–81; spelling, punctuation and grammar 83; spelling strategies 95; word reading 80

memory 18: and dyslexia 91–92; long-and short-term memory 1; phonological 23; and phonological awareness 23; and processing difficulties 47; verbal 21, 25, 27, 42, 63, 91; vulnerabilities 11; working memory see working memory; writing from 83
mental health first aid 101
mini-whiteboards to practice letter forms 71
mixing sounds 40
monitoring students 154
MOOCs 185
motor skills 54, 55, 71, 155; writing 59
multi-sensory support 101
music and drama: case study 65–66; Key Stage 1 65

National Curriculum for England 108
National Literacy Trust 190
neurodiversity 11
neurotypical individuals 162
non-fiction passages 82; reading 80
non-fiction texts 81
Northern Ireland 62, 130, 141; curriculum 109
Northern Ireland curriculum 109
Northern Ireland Dyslexia Centre 27

opacity of english 37–39
oracy skills 92
ordering and sequencing: dyslexia impacts, verbal memory 63; spelling strategies *64*
organisation skills 121
orthographic processing 18
orthographic skills 27

outside of literacy: different skills, knowledge and activities 62; impacts, dyslexia 62, 63; regions of UK 62

parents/carers 52, 78, 100–102, 113, 133, 135, 150, 192, 196; decision making 149; interview schedules for 3; potential support 76; support children at home 70, 190; support strategies 48; team 5; visual timetables and checklists 45; voice 145–146, *145*; and young people 138–141, 177
part-time study 165
passages: elements 89; make sense of 82; understanding, Key Stage 2 86; young people's understanding 81
patterns and orders 44–45
pen grips 71
person-first language 12
phonics and screener: EFYS to KS 1 *57*; EYFS 56; finding literacy tricky 56; formality of screener 56; Key Stage 1 56
phonics screener 56
phonics/speech-to-letter sounds: building blocks of English 70; developing literacy skills 70; English language 70; multiple speech or sound patterns 70; online programmes 70; programmes and support strategies 70; support children 71
phonological processing 18, 27
physical development 54; reading and writing 55
pictorial prompts, Key Stage 1 92
policy: changes 137; commonalities 137; English framework 137; Northern Ireland 141; parents/carers 138; practical strategies 142; and practices 136; roles and responsibilities 139; Scotland 140–141; SEND Code of Practice 137; stakeholders 139; teachers 139; terminology 137; Wales 140; young people 138
positive dyslexia 101–102, 184
post-compulsory pathways: caring responsibilities 160; case study 160–161; choosing what comes next 159; degree-apprenticeship 160; educators 160; GCSEs 159; post 16 pathways,

England 159; potential avenues 159; strengths and weaknesses with courses 160
practical support strategies: families struggle 189; literacy support 190; resources and strategies 190; routine and organisation support 190–191
primary to secondary shift: curriculum 107–110; differences 107; different types of institutions 105; impact, secondary school 107; memories 106; scools *106*; think of 106
processing information: challenges, verbal processing 92; classroom 92
processing speed 27, 47
Programme of Study for English 80, 83

reading: challenges 89; comprehension *see* reading comprehension; development 86; elements of 89; fluency 58; Key Stage 1 89; Key Stage 2 89; later primary school 89; reading and writing *see* reading and writing; and spelling *see* reading and spelling; understandings of topics 89; word *see* word reading
reading and spelling: deliver phonics, online packages 71; Key Stage 1 71; knowledge of 'shape' of language 71; using phonics 71
reading and writing: knowledge of phonics 55; physical development 55; skills 55; sound for letters 55; vulnerabilities 55
reading comprehension 57; expectations 58; Lower Key Stage 2 80–81; Upper Key Stage 2 82
reading problem: foundations of dyslexia 16; history of dyslexia 15; word blindness and dyslexia 16
reading skills: curriculum 80; end of Key Stage 1 80; image *81*; Key Stage 1 79; Key Stage 2 79; Lower Key Stage 2 80–81; reading comprehension 80; Upper Key Stage 2 81–82
reading strategies: audiobooks 97; individual 97; Lower Key Stage 2 97; paired reading 97; students' experiences of learning 98; support young people 97
reasoning skills 162
Reception Class 31, 34, 38

Reception Year 34
record: information, non-fiction texts 81; learning 90
remote or blended learning 165
rooms for different classes 114
The Rose Report 17
routine and organisation support 190–191

SASC and Delphi Study: BDA 24; cognitive challenges 24; cross-section of academics 22; design 22; impact 23; impairment/disability 23; manifestation 23; nature 23; phonological processing 23; time of writing 22; variance and co-occurrence 23; website 24
SATS 5, 96, 160
schoolbooks or notes 121
Scotland 27, 62, 130, 140; curriculum for excellence 110
Scottish statutory guidance 140
Scottish system 110
self-esteem 99
SEN Action 192
SEND Code of Practice 41, 72, 93, 101, 124, 137, 139, 154, 167, 168
SENDCOs 126, 139, 142, 144–146; qualifications 192; school 123
SEN framework 146
sense-making and time-taking: case study 43; verbal processing 42
sentences and clauses 83
sequences and patterns 42
sequencing and retaining information 91
short courses 185; and masters level 192; relating to dyslexia 184
short-term memory 91
size of writing 83
SLT and pastoral teams 113
social impact of dyslexia: confidence and self-esteem 122; conversations or ideas 122; externalised behaviour 123; keep up with others 121; knock-on effect on students 123; masking 122–123, *122*; mental health 123; plans 122; stigmatising characteristics 122
social model of disability 10
social model of dyslexia 13
sounds and letters: acquisition 38; bonkersness of english 39;

203

Index

challenges 38–39; complex spelling system, english 37–38; long 'a' 38; phonological awareness 38; vulnerabilities 38
sounds in words 54
spatial awareness 66
speaking and sounds 44
Special Educational Needs and Disability (SEND) 64, 129, 135, 137–139, 148, 177, 189, 191, 192; law 191, *191*; law course 193; policy 197; process 193; provision 109; structures 192; support 138; system 1, 146, 188
Specialist Assessor 69, 186; dyslexia 24; training 186
specific learning difficulties 13
specific learning disabilities 10
speech and language 53–54: ages of 3-4 children 33–35; babies and toddlers (0-3 years old) 33; difficulties 47; link *32*; make sense of the written word 36
speech for literacy 36
speech sounds in literacy: from 0–3 years old 36; children's phonological awareness 37; difficulties, children 44; direction of reading 37; writing in class *37*; written word and understand 37
spelling, punctuation and grammar: Lower Key Stage 2 83; Upper Key Stage 2 84
spelling 20; area of struggle and young people 90; and grammar 90; join letters 90; tests 98
spelling strategies: 3D, manipulable letters 95; colour coding patterns 95; dyslexia-friendly dictionaries 96; electronic dictionaries 96; forming letters 95; fridge magnets 95; Lower Key Stage 2 95; sandboxes 96; struggle, young people 95; tablet computers 96; Upper Key Stage 2 95; voice-activated responses 96
sports: children's experiences, school 64; clubs 194
stakeholder triad: agency and power 148–149; children's voice 142–144; development of relationships 133–134; parents/carers voice 145–146; positive interactions 135–136; relationships 149–150;

strengths, dyslexic individuals 172
strengths and likes after school 161–162
student loans 165
students support 154
success, conceptualisations of 154
summarisation 81
supporting literacy development: building blocks of 69; elements of literacy 69–70; phonics/speech-to-letter sounds 70–71, *70*; reading and spelling 71; writing 71–72

tablet computers, standard spelling 96
teaching strategies 185
time: support children and families 180, 182; supporting young people 197
timetable and subjects: challenges for teachers and students 114; curriculum impacts 110; primary school 111; secondary schools 112; secondary school *versus* primary school 110; T-levels 167–168
toddler-hood 33
training 183
Tribunal process 192

understanding instructions 66–67
unexpected sounds and spellings 80
universal design for learning 178–179
university/a degree 165
university/universities 66, 185; accept T Levels 167
Upper Key Stage 2: handwriting and composition 84–86; reading comprehension 82; spelling, punctuation and grammar 84; spelling strategies 95; word reading 81–82

verbal memory 21, 25, 27, 42, 63, 91
verbal processing 45, 92; challenges 99
visual instructions 66–67, *67*
visual thinking skills 66
vocational: apprenticeships 167; classified 166; different routes *166*; T levels and other qualifications 167–168; vocational pathway 166
vulnerabilities: handwriting 84; impact on academic attainment 1; organisation skills 121; reading and writing 55; spoken word 40; verbal processing 45, 92; working memory 121

weaknesses: desks and learning 54; memory 92; short-term memory 91; students 121; working memory 91
wellbeing: and boosting child 72; mental health 99–100; neurodiversities 99;
Welsh Code of Practice 140
Welsh education system 109
WESFORD 102
word reading: EYFS experiences and expectations 58; EYFS Learning Goals 57; fluency 58; Key Stage 1 57; literacy strugggles *60*; Lower Key Stage 2 80; ordering of the skill areas 57; phonics knowledge 57; spoken language 57; Upper Key Stage 2 81–82; use of apostrophes 57; wider curriculum 60–62; writing and spelling 58–59; young people 57
working and part-time study 165
working changes and expectations 114–118; case studies 115–118; challenges in literacy 114; good and bad, school *118*; interviews with families 115; relationships and communication 118; secondary school 114
working memory 1, 18, 23, 24, 27, 45, 55, 59, 60, 63, 79, 87, 91, 95, 101, 102, *120*, 121, 125, 170, 197; capacity 121; challenges, early years 42; sequences and patterns 42; vulnerabilities 121; young people 120; zone out 121
working with dyslexic children 183–184
workplace and post-school settings 154
workshops for DT 114
work things to consider 172

World Health Organisation 15, 18, 21
writing 57; alternative recording strategie 72; areas 57; basic ideas, letter formation 71; development 86; different forms of 84; and dyslexia 90, *91*; juggling spellings and word order 92; physical act of letter formation 71; planning skills 72; planning strategies 96–97, *97*; process of 71; sentence-starters 72;
writing and spelling: challenges 59; dictation 59; handwriting expectations 59; Key Stage 1 curriculum 58; vulnerabilities in working memory 59
writing/planning strategies: 96
writing practice classes/groups 71
writing tasks 91
written word 86

young people: develop positive attitudes to reading 80; with dyslexia, academics 162; gross motor skills 54; secondary school *see* secondary school; working and part-time study 165
young people support: challenges 194; Complete University Guide, dyslexic students 195; moving on and moving up *196*; recruitment website 195; sense of solidarity and community 194; social media 194; thread on the 'Student Room' 194; TikTok 194; time management 195; work with older individuals 193

zone out, working memory 121

For Product Safety Concerns and Information please contact our EU
representative GPSR@taylorandfrancis.com
Taylor & Francis Verlag GmbH, Kaufingerstraße 24, 80331 München, Germany

www.ingramcontent.com/pod-product-compliance
Lightning Source LLC
Chambersburg PA
CBHW072232240426
43670CB00040B/2503